A Journey Through the Heavens

A Journey Through the Heavens

MY NEAR-DEATH EXPERIENCES
AND AFTEREFFECTS

A SPIRITUAL MEMOIR

Tina Wrassmann

AVAILABLE LIGHT PRESS
Maineville, Ohio

This work is a memoir. It depicts actual events in the life of the author as truthfully as recollection permits. The names and identifying details of some of the individuals mentioned in this book have been changed to protect their privacy.

Copyright © Tina Wrassmann, 2022

All rights reserved. No part of this book may be reproduced or used in any manner without the prior written permission of the copyright owner, except for the use of brief quotations in a book review.

Printed in the United States of America.

ISBN: 979-8-9866486-0-6 (paperback)
ISBN: 979-8-9866486-1-3 (ebook)

Library of Congress Control Number: 2022943434

Cover Design by nskvsky

Scripture quotation is from the ESV® Bible (The Holy Bible, English Standard Version®), copyright © 2001 by Crossway, a publishing ministry of Good News Publishers. Used by permission. All rights reserved.

Scripture quotations marked (NIV) are taken from the Holy Bible, New International Version®, NIV®. Copyright © 1973, 1978, 1984, 2011 by Biblica, Inc.™ Used by permission of Zondervan. All rights reserved worldwide. www.zondervan.com. The "NIV" and "New International Version" are trademarks registered in the United States Patent and Trademark Office by Biblica, Inc.™

First Edition

Published by Available Light Press, Maineville, Ohio.

www.availablelightpress.com

To the Lord *God Almighty—*
may this honor and glorify You.

and

To my children—
may the Lord *richly bless you in all you do.*

"God is spirit, and those who worship him must worship in spirit and truth."
—John 4:24

Contents

Preface xi
Introduction xiii

PART 1: MY FIRST NEAR-DEATH EXPERIENCE

1. An Unexpected Journey 3
2. Integration 14
3. Interpretations, Explanations and Lessons 17
4. Scriptural Connections 46

PART 2: MY SECOND NEAR-DEATH EXPERIENCE

5. To a Council and Back 55
6. Integration 58
7. Interpretations, Explanations and Lessons 61
8. Scriptural Connections 69

PART 3: OTHER SPIRITUAL ENCOUNTERS

9. What in Heaven Has Happened to Me? 75
10. My Neighbor's Golden Glow 80
11. My Unborn Child 82

12. A Comforting Angel 84
13. Curious Onlookers 87
14. Spirits in My House 88
15. My Mother's Death 91
16. My Husband's Death 93
17. The Death of a Childhood Friend 95
18. An Angel at a Funeral 97
19. A Spirit Masking as My Mother 98
20. An Angel's Offer 100
21. You Are Sealed 102
22. Two Slithery Spirits 105
23. Charismatic Church Visit 107
24. Baby Gender and Name 109
25. Conclusion 112
For My Father 115

PREFACE

The unexpected happens, but I never thought it would happen to me. It was not only unexpected but surreal. My first near-death experience occurred in 1964 when I was 26 years old. A second one occurred 11 years later. This book is about these experiences and their aftereffects. It is a compilation of my experiences in the unseen spiritual realm up to the present time.

As I finish this book, I am 84 years old. By the grace of God, I have not lost a step in my cognitive function. I still drive my car, visit with friends, grocery shop, and pick up my five-year-old grandson and hold him. I say these things because the details of my two near-death experiences and host of other spiritual encounters have not faded in my memory. To the contrary, they are just as real to me and fresh in my mind as the days I had them. They continue to be a surprise as I encounter them.

Parts of the book were written early on. Explanations of the events, however, were written recently. The original manuscript was intended only for my family, but I decided that releasing it publicly could offer hope and encouragement to many. It is important to know that our spirits do live on after physical death, that there is a God who loves and cares for us, and that there is indeed an unseen spiritual realm.

My near-death experiences were such that the beings I encountered during them met me where I was at the time in my spiritual development and understanding. They gave me the knowledge and insight I needed concerning my religious questions as well as for my life purposes. They often schooled me with their answers, at times in a rebuking manner. It was more like teacher-student relationships in realms of love, truth, beauty, absolute security, and the absence of fear. I have tried to be as faithful as possible in representing these sentiments in writing, and I realize that doing so colors my experiences with a more serious tone rather than one of all warm and happy feelings, which one may or may not expect in a book about a journey to heaven.

The physical realm and the spiritual realm are connected. Thanks to the mercy and kindness of our Creator, I have seen and experienced both. The Creator is truly the Father of our spirits and loves us with an unconditional love.

Come along with me and see what I have seen.

Tina Wrassmann
September 2, 2022

Introduction

An Initial Awakening

My father passed away when I was five years old. It was the custom in our family to have friends over the night before the visitation at the funeral home. A friend of the family picked me up and sat me on her lap. She was trying to explain my father's death to me. She said that God had taken my father to heaven because he really needed him. I did not understand that because God had everything. I was the one who needed my father. I could not understand why God would take him from me. But God took him anyway. I hated God because of that.

At the funeral service, another one of my mother's friends carried me in her arms to my father's casket. She told me to kiss his hand. I did. His hand was cold. That is all I remember about my father's funeral.

The next few years went by, and during that time I lived with an emptiness inside me. I attended the public school nearby. I always felt different from my schoolmates because they all had a father. But I did not. When I turned nine years old, my mother decided I was old enough to cross streets without crossing guards, so she sent my brother and me to a Catholic school about a fifteen-minute walk from home.

Things went well at the new school, but I still had that emptiness within me. It was like an ache. When I was in the sixth grade, the pastor of the church taught us a class on church history. Then, something unusual happened. The pastor began explaining what church history was about and then made an unrelated and surprising comment. He said that if a child had lost his or her father, God then became the child's father. He looked at no one in particular when he said it, but I remember thinking it was directed to me because I did not know of anyone else in my class who had lost their father. His comment stuck with me.

On the way home from school that same day, I waited for the red traffic light to change to green at an intersection, and that is where I decided to accept the pastor's comment as the truth. It was at that precise moment that I had a spiritual awakening in accepting God as my Father—my heavenly Father. I now had a Father. Immediately, the deep, empty ache inside me closed and vanished. I was whole again. I was ashamed that I had ever hated God, my Father. Then, the light turned green, and I walked home. The emptiness has never returned.

A Falling Out

I attended Catholic schools from the fifth grade through high school. When I was 13 years old, doubts surfaced about some of the Catholic Church's teachings. The most important issue concerned the Bible. At that time, we were not allowed to read it because a priest would need to interpret it for us. We were, however, permitted to read the snippets of scripture found in our Missals given to us at our Confirmation ceremony. Since our faith rested on the Bible's teachings, I found all this unbelievably upsetting. If the Bible was the word of God to his people, then we should not only be able to read it from beginning to end ourselves, but to understand it as well.

Introduction

My first near-death experience happened during my Roman Catholic years, several months before my marriage. One major lesson I learned during that near-death experience was that there is a big difference between faith and organized religion. What exactly was the difference? I needed to find that out and thus began my quest to find the truth of faith versus religion. Where else could I find the answer but in reading the Bible? It is the basis of Christianity. Eventually, I left the Catholic Church, but I did not leave my Christian faith.

A Spiritual Redirection

Spurred by my first near-death experience, although several years later, I completed my goal to read the Bible. I read it not only once but twice. A dream I had also served as encouragement for me to do this. In the dream, I saw a large open door in the sky. It was one very thick, single door. It began to close on its own. I became quite anxious because I thought that heaven was closing its door, and no one would ever be able to enter again once it was shut. I immediately streamed toward the door. Just as it was closing, I squeezed through the opening before it slammed shut with a loud bang. I woke up startled and in a cold sweat.

After this dream and with Bible knowledge now under my belt, I felt I had enough discernment to find a church for our young family. My husband and I found one that was devoted to reading through the Bible each year, with weekly Sunday sermons on that week's subject. This is when all things spiritual really began to converge within me, and I began to have a focused spiritual life.

As time passed, we moved on to experience other Protestant churches but never settled on any one specific denomination. Nevertheless, I always remained an active Christian.

Through all this, my two near-death experiences have been

extremely significant pillars in my spiritual life. They have served both as catalysts for spiritual growth and major corrections for my life path and journey. My life would perhaps be very different without them. They have revealed to me great purpose, wisdom, and understanding of what it means to be a human being, and just what we're doing here on the earth.

My near-death experiences and other spiritual encounters have been the colorful flash to an otherwise mostly normal life and Christian walk—raising kids, a Sunday sermon, a Bible study, a prayer group, a journey through the heavens, spirits walking through my house, my unborn child appearing at the foot of my bed. You know, the typical Christian walk, right? *Riiiiight*. And now I turn to these.

Part 1

My First Near-Death Experience

1

AN UNEXPECTED JOURNEY

It was a Friday afternoon in the spring of 1964, and I had an appointment with my allergist. I was taking a series of injections to build up my immunity to various grasses and weeds. I left work half an hour early that day to keep my appointment. This was to be the second to last injection. I was relieved that it was almost over because there was always swelling at the injection site which was uncomfortable for a couple of days.

After I was given the injection, I sat in the waiting room for about ten minutes to make sure there was no adverse reaction, per normal. All of a sudden, I started feeling unwell. I felt a burning heat start at my waist and radiate down my legs. I got up immediately and walked over to the receptionist. I told her I thought I was having a reaction. She asked me to follow her back to an examination room just around the corner from the waiting room. Just as we turned the corner, the heat radiated through my whole body. I began to burn up, my knees became weak, and I slowly fell to the floor in a faint. The floor was covered with vinyl tile, and the last thing I remembered was how cool it felt against my hot cheek.

When I opened my eyes, I was lying on a table in an examination room with my doctor standing to my right near my head. I felt so bad. I closed my eyes. The thought occurred to me that I was dying. I folded my hands on my abdomen and then heard the doctor say that I was not going to die. *Yes*, I thought, *I am. I am dying.*

The First Heaven

The next moment I found myself, my consciousness, outside my body and at the ceiling in the right-hand corner of the room. I looked back to see myself, and the doctor was still standing by my head between the wall and my body. Another person was standing opposite him by my left foot.

The very next moment, the room was gone. I was in a dark grey area standing on top of a table. The table was made of concrete and rested on a pedestal. It was round in shape. I did not see it. I somehow knew what it looked like in my mind.

I was encased in what seemed to me to be a dense, grey fog and could not see anything around me. I saw no walls, nothing. I did not like it. I knew I would have to leave that place. I thought to myself that I had to figure out where I was going. *I know*, I thought, *I am going to God.* I looked to my left and then to my right. It was lighter to my right, so I decided I would go in that direction. I tried turning to the right, but my feet were stuck to the table, as if I were not allowed to just go in any direction. The table, however, made a half turn to my right anyway, on its own.

Suddenly out of nowhere, I heard a sound like jet engines rushing toward me. Two entities that I perceived to be angels appeared to my left. I say perceived because I was not allowed to see them fully as they were, though I could sense them.

One of them told me that I was not expected but they had received a message to come to me, and came as soon as they could. He seemed apologetic that they had not arrived sooner because they were at work elsewhere. He asked me where I was going. His question perplexed and surprised me because, as angels, I expected them to know where I was going. So, I answered in a surprised voice, "Why, I am going to God!" The angels then positioned themselves behind me, one on each side, and immediately the table turned back to its original orientation. Each angel had one hand on my back and propelled me upwards. I did not feel the hands. I only knew that it was so.

As we streamed upwards, it seemed to take a very long time. While we were moving, the area we went through continued to be like a dense, grey fog. To my left the darkness seemed to have hardened. I wondered, as we were streaming alongside it, if it was a wall. As time passed, I began to wonder when we would ever get there. One of the angels told me to look for the light. As I looked, I saw a tiny white pinpoint of light which, as we kept ascending, became larger. It looked like a portal.

When we reached the opening, I wondered if the three of us could get through it together. I went through the opening first, and then, concerned, turned around to see if they were going to get through. I watched as they came through safely together. The opening had enlarged itself to accommodate them.

The Second Heaven

We entered into a very bright realm of light. My first impression was of amazement at the brightness of the light shining so strongly, brighter than the sun. I wondered why it did not hurt my eyes. And this made me wonder if I even had eyes. I squeezed my eyes shut as tightly as possible to see if I could feel my eyelashes. I could, and decided that I did still have eyes.

And then to my surprise and amazement, pieces of armor began flying off me, piece by piece. It started at my left shoulder, and then they all disappeared into the atmosphere. I didn't know I had on armor. Once freed from it, I became joyously happy and light as a bird. I did flip flops and somersaults in the air and flew around. It was absolutely wonderful. I had no fears, anxieties, or worries. I was totally free and unencumbered.

Next, I wondered what I was wearing. I looked down to see the brightest, whitest gown I had ever seen. It glistened. It was so bright that the bottom edges, which covered my feet, were obliterated by shards of light radiating out from the hem of the garment.

At this point we began to fly over an earth-like landscape. The colors were so vibrantly beautiful. As we flew lower, I saw a family of four on a picnic in a pastoral setting on a hilltop. The mother had a red and white checkered tablecloth in her hands. She was shaking it out to place it on the grass while it billowed in the breeze. Her husband and two children, one girl and one boy, both with dark hair, were with her. I wondered if they were my family, but on closer inspection they were not.

I then looked in the far distance and saw a fence. It seemed to be a division line between two properties. Behind the fence I saw a couple of four-footed farm animals that looked like a horse and a donkey because of their shape and size, but I was not sure because they were blurred. There were undulating hills in the distance. The grass was the most beautiful and vibrant color of green. A beautiful blue lake sat nearby. The sky was light blue, clear and cloudless. The day was bright with light.

As we continued our journey flying through the sky, I wondered if I had ever done anything wrong, since I was going to God. In that instant, I saw ahead of me a large, clear globe. The angel told me without words that I was in that globe. I interpreted this to mean that my soul was in that globe. I hurried up to it and found an opening on the opposite side. It was more of an indentation. I stepped in with my left foot and peered around into the opening. I looked all around it and could see through it, but there was nothing in it. My immediate thought was that I had never done anything wrong. I wondered if that was how God saw me since Jesus died for our sins.

To me, that meant that now I had to figure out what good things I had done so I could tell God. But when I told this to the angel upon exiting the globe, the angel told me in no uncertain terms that my good deeds were like filthy rags. He said there was only one who was good, and that was God. And then he showed me a small squirrel standing in comparison to the earth.

As we continued on, I thought that I must try and remember some scriptures, but the only one that came to mind was that God "is all and in all." I asked the angel what that scripture meant. Immediately, I was transported to what I thought was the earth, and my eyes were at grass level. It was autumn, and we were in the woods. I looked around and saw grass on the ground, and a small green bush to my left. I looked to see if there was a fire in the bush, but there was not. A tree was a little to my right, and close by, so that we were almost under it. The tree was dropping its beautifully colored leaves to the ground, and a breeze was scattering them. I mentioned the dead leaves to the angel, and he said, "They are not dead, they are alive!" He continued and said, "God is in all of it, even the leaves, which seem dead because they are brown, orange, and gold. They are not dead, because God is in them. And God, Jesus, who is in them, is what holds everything together." He paused for a moment, then continued, "If he stops thinking about us for even a moment, we will no longer exist." The way he said this made me think this included everything created, even him.

Anytime I wanted to know something, I was immediately answered, but not by any particular, audible voice. The answers were impressed upon me through the top of my head, like mental telepathy. This seemed to come from above, starting at my head, and going all the way down to my feet, like I absorbed it. I asked and was answered immediately.

By this time, we had traveled quite a long way, and I wondered where we were in the universe. I turned around to my left and looked over my shoulder hoping to get a glimpse of the two angels, but they stayed attached behind me, outside my vision. I inspected the sky looking for something familiar, like the earth, but it was nowhere in sight. I looked for our planets, which I thought would be lined up in a row, but they were not there. There was nothing but space. I did see one star, however, a little to my right and in the very faraway distance. I could see partially through it. Outside of that one star, there was nothing but immense space and grey sky as far as I could see. I turned back around, and we continued flying on our journey through this atmosphere.

At this point, I could hear my heart beating loudly. Therefore, I knew that my body back on earth was not in a final state of death. It was so loud that it filled my whole being.

I asked another question in my mind, something I really wanted to know. *What are the building blocks of creation?* There was no immediate answer. Then all of a sudden, we were at the edge of a high mountain looking out into space. Jesus was in the distance. He was lying down on his back and looked like a huge, carved, wooden statue. The whole world was within him. This confused me. I then wondered where I was in him, and the answer came—in his side.

We continued moving along and came to a plane, or dome, right above us. We floated under it for a short time until we came to an opening. Just as I was going around the plane and before I stepped up onto it, I took a good look at it. It was a dark gold color, like gold mixed with an alloy, maybe brass. I did not know for sure. The surface was hammered in appearance. I wondered what the light would look like reflected on it from a distance. The dome was thin, and on top of it was about an inch of dirt, and grass grew on top of that. As I stepped up onto it, I wondered if it would hold my weight. It did.

The Third Heaven

I was now on a dirt road in a farm-like setting. The open vastness of the universe expanded off to my right. A park sat to my left. A man was sitting on a concrete bench, his back toward me. He had a child on his lap. I could not see the child except for its very straight back and light brown, slightly curly, short hair. The child was about the size of a three-year-old. The man seemed to know I was there because he slowly turned and looked at me. The next thing I knew, he was standing on the grass at the edge of the road. An angel arrived to tend to the child. I asked him if the child was me. He smiled, slightly shook his head and said no. I did not hear his voice though.

His eyes were full of such kindness. When he looked at me, he captured my full attention. He seemed to know me, but I did not know who he was, and I could tell he knew that. I asked him if he was my father. He paused a moment, turned his head to his left as if listening to someone give him information, then looked back at me and again shook his head no. He was small in stature compared to men today. Strangely, I seemed to grow a little taller while looking at him. He smiled, and his brown eyes twinkled. He seemed to know something happy about me that I did not know. Suddenly, he was somehow pulled away backward into the park, and I watched until he disappeared.

When I turned back to the road, I saw it—at long last, I saw it. The heavenly city! It was enshrouded in a cloud, except for one room that protruded out of the cloud. The room had a curved glass or some kind of see-through material around it. A deep chasm, which went off to the left, separated me from the heavenly city. I looked into the chasm to see if Abraham was there, but he was not.

I sensed one of the angels near me. The angel asked if I thought I could jump over the chasm. I was not to fall into it. I would have to jump over it if I wanted to look in the room, and then decide if I wanted to go in. If I decided I wanted to go in, I would need to return back over the chasm from where I had just come, and then make my final decision. I said I thought I could jump over it. At this point, I heard my heart beating again. And just as before when I heard my heart beating, I knew I was not yet fully dead.

I easily jumped over the chasm and was on the other side. I stood there marveling as I looked down and saw that I had on a long gown. I had also retained the slightly increased height given to me in my interaction with the man on the park bench. I looked back across the chasm, and the large globe I had seen earlier was there. Two eyes were in it and were watching me. It was true what the angel had said to me before—I was in that globe. I turned away and proceeded up to the window to look inside.

The window was the width of the room. There were flowers inside, under the window, and it was raining inside. The flowers were of various colors and looked to be made out of carved wood, just like how I had seen Jesus. The length of the room was about twice its width. It reminded me of a room in a flower conservatory. There was a hallway down the middle of the room that went off to the right. I sensed there was a door there into the rest of this structure.

The rain and flowers puzzled me. I looked to see if there was some sort of sprinkling system at the ceiling because the rain was coming down from above, but there was none. Why would rain be falling in a house where there were flowers carved of wood? They could not absorb the water. Where did the water go? Outside of that, the room looked safe enough, and I decided I would like to go in. I wanted to walk through the door that went into the inner part of the building.

Before I could do that, however, I needed to return over the chasm to where I started, as the angel had instructed me, and make my final decision there. So, I returned. I wanted entry into that room. I then tried jumping over the chasm for the second time, but I encountered a force field now in place and was bounced back onto the ground. I got up immediately with the intention of trying a third time. But at that point and to my utter amazement, instead of looking up to where I would be going, I was looking at myself, my small spirit in the white dress. The small spirit was now jumping higher than I had over the chasm. It bounced off the force field and was propelled back across the chasm. It came bouncing back toward me and entered right into me between my ribs. We were one once again.

At that moment, a sudden strong wind turned me around. I was surrounded by six angels, three on each side. We hurriedly moved forward as the wind at my back pushed me down the dirt road. A white fence sat to my right along the road with a few green bushes growing behind it, a little sparse grass here and there, and a tree in the distance. It looked barren and desolate. The tree had only a few brown leaves on it. The ground sloped behind it, like this area was on a hillside. Then I heard the sound of someone's mocking laughter coming from the sky above the fenced area as we moved along. I did not like that.

We were nearing the area where I had seen the man on the bench, and I hoped I would see him again. I looked for him in the park-like setting, but he was not there. The bench and the child were also gone.

An angel was standing at the opening where I had originally entered. A white sheet was tied on either side of the ground in front of me, kind of like a slide shaped like a hammock. The angel pointed to the sheet with an outstretched arm and an encouraging demeanor, waiting for me to get on it; this was to take me back to the earth realm. But I was apprehensive. Nevertheless, I jumped on the sheet and slid down.

Back to Earth

I landed, seated on the floor, in the hallway of the doctor's office near the room where my body was located. The two angels who had accompanied me on my journey hovered over me. I felt that there were loving spirits all around me, more than just the two.

One of the angels who was with me from the beginning knelt down to my level, one knee up and one knee down, so we were face to face. The other angel who was with me from the beginning was now behind me. I sensed his wings were spread as if to protect me and the area behind me. I told the angel in front of me that I wanted to know if the doctor who had given me the injection would be held responsible for what he had done. The angel said, "No, he will not be held responsible, he will be held accountable."

I also told him I never wanted my spirit to be that small again. And what must I do with my life, I wanted to know? He held an open book in his hand, which he looked at intently. He then looked back up at me. I wondered to myself if it was the Book of Life, but decided it was not. I was becoming distracted now because I could see my body which was facing the open door at the end of the hallway. My body seemed to pull me toward it like a magnet. I could not make out what the angel was saying between that and some noisy interference like static. I only knew he was trying to tell me something about a book—whether I was to write a book, read a book, start a book club, I did not know.

As I looked down the hall, I saw six angels, three on each side of the short hallway, with their faces toward the wall and their wings spread, touching each other. I was then next to my body and then above my body. I carefully fit myself into my body. I did not remember seeing either my hands or feet during my time out-of-body, so I lifted each to make sure they were there and worked, and they did. I also realized that my heartbeat was no longer pounding in my ears. However, I did not feel quite back to my normal self.

As I was getting reoriented, a man peered around the door to look at me. He saw that I was conscious. He walked into the room and introduced himself. He was a cardiologist, and he and my doctor had offices next to each other and shared the waiting room.

He explained he had been tending me for the past hour and a half, and had administered a shot of adrenaline to keep my heart beating. He told me I had gone into diastolic shock and had no blood pressure. He also told me the adrenaline made me alternately hot and cold, and that he had been covering me with a blanket or removing it as necessary when he checked on me in between seeing his patients. He told me that another of my doctor's patients also had a reaction, but he had already left, and so had my doctor. He went on to say that I was free to go home when my body returned to normal in about fifteen minutes. Just then, I started to shake with a chill, and he covered me with the blanket as I blacked out.

I don't know how long I was out after that, but when I opened my eyes, I felt like myself again. A couple of minutes later, the cardiologist came back into the room. I assume he checked my vital signs because he gave me permission to leave and said I would be fine. His parting words were to eat pretzels and drink lots of water.

I stayed home from work the next day, but had no ill effects, except for the allergy injection site, which was slightly swollen and pink in color.

2

INTEGRATION

The day of my near-death experience, my appointment with my allergist was at 5:00 pm. It took me about five minutes or so to get home, which was around 7:00 pm. I was unconscious for an hour and fifteen minutes according to my calculation. I thought what happened while I was unconscious was just a dream, though one that I could remember in vivid detail.

For a long time afterward, I felt like two people, as if I had somehow been split in two. Part of me was very aware of the experience, and I was now trying to integrate it into my every day existence. As time passed, I decided that I could not do it, so I made the decision to ignore it and just live my life. I told myself it was only a dream. I never told anyone about it for many years.

In 1969, when the book *On Death and Dying* by Elisabeth Kubler-Ross was published, I read it. That is when I realized my dream was not a dream but actually very much like the out-of-body experiences described in the book. Those experiences often occurred while people were unconscious after a traumatic experience. My experience was like that also. There was now no question that I had some sort of out-of-body experience. Up until that time, I had never heard of such a thing.

Once I realized what really had happened to me, clarity soon followed. I came to the conclusion that I had a spiritual life separate from my human life, but both within me, and they influence each other. The confusing part was that when they conflict, I must make the choice of which way to go—and hence, the inability to integrate them.

It has taken decades to understand and integrate my experience. Writing it all down has allowed me an overall view of its immense significance. It has also helped me understand the love God has for his sons and daughters created in his image.

Raymond Moody, the one who coined the phrase, "near-death experience," wrote the book *Life After Life*. His book has been very helpful to me. Moody lists 15 criteria for a near-death experience based on interviews with people who experienced them. Not everyone has all 15 criteria, but they have many of them in common. My experience falls under his definition.

Over the years, I have learned all the things I needed to learn from my near-death experience to put me on the right track regarding my faith and religious beliefs. Specifically, I found out that I am accountable to God for everything I do. When I die, no human being will go along with me to eternity; we each go alone. In addition, I learned I needed to know where I was going when I died. Also, I learned that the answer to what is expected of me in order to enter heaven is found in the Bible. My human life on earth prepares me for the reality of eternity based on my earthly experiences, but I must also have a spiritual life. It is my choice how I will live in eternity, that is, either with or without God. In order to do this, I must have a spiritual life because God is a spirit. My spiritual life must overcome my own physicality in striving to live righteously, which is so often spoken about and defined in the Bible.

Another noteworthy aspect of the experience is that I never once had any fear. I do not have any fear of dying now. Death is merely a transition from one state of being to another. And it happens in an instant. Saying that, however, I must add the caveat that I hope to die in my sleep. I have no fear of death itself, just how it happens.

The most important result from this experience was the decision to purchase a Bible and read it from cover to cover. I had never read it before. It was in the late 1970s when I actually opened it and began to read it. When I read Genesis 1 and came to the third verse, I found the answer to the question I asked the angel, "What are the building blocks of creation?" It says, "And God said, 'Let there be light,' and there was light" (Genesis 1:3). It was words! God's words, and on the very first page. I sometimes wondered if there was a substance God had already created from nothing which he used to make the heavens and the earth and which complied perfectly with his spoken commands. No mention of that was in the biblical text.

In my life, I had tried all the options I mentioned to the angel as I was leaving him. I started a book club, and it was fun, but it was not the answer. I started writing a book about the watcher angels, but that did not go anywhere. Reading the Bible was the only one of my three choices that satisfied me. It gave me peace with myself. It showed me the truth, and after all, that was all I ever wanted.

One surprising thing during my journey is when I progressed into the Second Heaven, I never once had a thought about any of my family or friends (I did, however, wonder if the family in the picnic scene in the earth-like landscape was my family). It was as if they had been expunged from my memory. One way I can explain this is that throughout this experience no one else was ever mentioned or alluded to. The lessons learned were geared only to my needs. It was a major course correction for my life spiritually which affected my life on earth as a human being. How we live and what we do on earth matters and has eternal significance.

Since then, my life has changed in many ways. One of the aftereffects is that a door was opened into the unseen spiritual world, and I am very aware of its existence. In Part 3, I will go into detail of my many experiences.

3

INTERPRETATIONS, EXPLANATIONS AND LESSONS

All my earthly experiences up to the time of my near-death experience were the backdrop used to help explain what I was seeing and hearing (without spoken words from me or the angels) on this spiritual journey. We communicated telepathically through our minds.

There were two angels accompanying me. However, it seemed that communication to me came from the same one each time. The angel explained nothing unless I asked, and when he answered, I understood and accepted it as the absolute truth and did not question him. It never entered my mind that anything unusual was happening to me.

I have used the following four-stage synopsis as the basis for the interpretations, explanations and lessons that follow. This synopsis will lend clarity to the structure of the experience.

Synopsis

The first stage took place in a dark spiritual realm, which I call the First Heaven. The main items here are: my spirit leaving my body; being on a large pedestal; meeting two guiding angels; and being taken upward through the First Heaven toward a portal or light.

The second stage took place in the Second Heaven once through the portal. The main items here are: moving through the portal; experiencing the light; shedding my outer armor; being dressed in a white dress; flying above a pastoral scene with greatly enhanced colors; seeing a family on a picnic on a hillside and animals in the distance; seeing my soul; being admonished by an angel about good deeds; an explanation to a question about God being all in all which included an autumn-like scene; seeing only a lonely star in the sky; hearing my heart beating very loudly; asking about the building blocks of creation/the wooden statue of Jesus; and approaching the Third Heaven.

The third stage took place in the Third Heaven after I had approached its underbelly and stepped up onto it. The main items here are: the Third Heaven's thin metal floor covered with dirt and grass; a man and child in a park-like setting; the entrance to God's dwelling place/city that was partially hidden behind a cloud; my heart beating loudly; looking into a room; my small spirit; not being allowed to enter; passing by a fenced-in field as a wind propelled me to this heaven's exit; hearing mocking laughter; and being sent back down to the earth realm on a slide made out of a sheet that was shaped like a hammock.

The fourth stage took place back on earth in the location of the building which housed my doctor's office. The main items here are: landing on the hallway floor of the doctor's office; speaking with the angel; the hallway of angels; my spirit moving back into my body.

The First Stage: First Heaven

My Spirit Leaving My Body

When I thought to myself that I was dying, I meant it. Instantly, I was at the ceiling looking back at my body on the gurney. The transition was instant and painless. I remember turning my head around to look back and noted a person standing by my left foot. That was unexpected. I had not realized someone had been there. But I had no feelings about it one way or the other. And then, abruptly, I was gone from the room.

Pedestal Table

Because it was so dark, I did not actually see what the pedestal table looked like, but knew that was what I was standing on. It reminded me of a sundial because of its shape, and also because I was placed there and could not move my feet, a stopping point.

The sundial is the ancient way to tell time based on the shadow that the sun, or light, makes on the dial as it traverses the sky. I was like the dial casting its shadow to tell the time. However, it was dark and I was not casting a shadow. Time had stopped for me. I went from being surrounded by a dense, grey cloud, not unlike the color of a shadow, into the light, and no longer under the constraints of time or gravity.

Because my feet were stuck to the top of the table, I was going nowhere. This reminded me of people waiting for a bus or train that will take them to their destination, but until it arrives, they have to wait, whether they like it or not. I was waiting in the opaque darkness for my guiding angels to take me to my destination, though I did not know that at the time. But they did.

Another symbolic meaning is how we tend to put people on a pedestal who are held in high esteem for various reasons and are beloved. God holds his children in high esteem, in fact, all of his creation. I could have been placed anywhere, but I found myself on a pedestal. That is where God positioned me and kept me safe until his guiding angels came to me. They knew the way through the heavens to my destination, which I did not.

The tabletop turned in the direction I wanted to go on its own. I do not know how that happened. Why it happened, though, is because the angels were coming to me from that direction. When the tabletop stopped turning, I heard the sound the angels made in flight. The sound was reminiscent of jet engines, almost as if they were announcing themselves ahead of their arrival, perhaps so I would look toward the sound and see them.

If my original position on the tabletop faced me toward the north, then the angels came to me from the east. When they positioned themselves behind me, the tabletop turned back to its original position. The three of us then went straight up, not right or left, or forward or backward. That was not a direction I would have thought possible, at least not on earthly terms.

I do not know how my feet became unattached to the tabletop, nor how the table returned to its original position. The angels must have taken care of that, but they did not communicate it to me.

The Two Angels

The two angels who were sent to guide me had form and substance. One of them questioned me just like someone on earth would have done, except no verbal words were exchanged between us. I heard the words in my mind, telepathically, and my mind answered just as if I had spoken. They were right in front of me in the opaque darkness, but I do not know what they actually looked like and cannot describe them. I do not think the reason for that was just the darkness surrounding the three of us. It was not meant for me to see what they looked like.

Moving Upward through the First Heaven Toward a Portal

As we were streaming upward, I began to wonder when we would ever get to where they were taking me because it was taking so long. One of the angels told me to look for the light. I never would have known to do that. It seems that I had to think specifically about the light in order to find it. We now know based on many other near-death experience accounts that moving toward the light is a typical occurrence; however, this was virtually unknown when I had my near-death experience. Looking for the light is an important concept because it begs the question, do we get what we expect? If so, we had better know what to expect. I saw a pinpoint of light almost immediately, and it made me so happy. As it loomed larger, the light came from a portal but did not extend outside it. In size, it reminded me of a manhole cover on earth.

The Second Stage: Second Heaven

Moving Through the Portal

Since the three of us had been joined together through the ascent from the beginning, I assumed we would go through the portal together. But the portal was too small for that, so I was concerned. However, I need not have worried. I went through first then turned around to see them come through together. I was in awe to see that the portal had enlarged itself to accommodate them. We had gone from the darkness into the light. Also, they were now no longer attached to me.

This portal brings up an interesting question: is the only way to go from the First Heaven into the Second Heaven through a portal? Was the opened portal somehow connected to my thought of it? The portal did not appear until the angel told me to look for the light. We were flying upward for some time through the dark First Heaven. How much longer would we have flown if I hadn't looked for the light? To me, this suggests that the portal from the First Heaven into the second was somehow connected to my thought process, or state of being. The angels knew where to go. But I did not. I knew where I wanted to go, but not how to get there. They were waiting for me to look for the light.

Experiencing the Light

The second heaven is a realm of light. The first heaven is not. This is why the portal was so starkly obvious (once I was told to look for it) while streaming upward through it to the Second Heaven. During this time, I could sense all that was around me. This heightened sense came from being in the spirit.

On entering the second heavenly realm, I was in awe of the brightness of the light. I can only describe this light as the light of God, although I could not detect specifically where it was coming from. It was much brighter than any light I had experienced on earth, but it did not hurt my eyes. I remember looking up at the sky. Unlike earth, there was no sun or clouds. That is why I have assumed the light emanated from God himself in the Third Heaven.

On earth I always wore sunglasses when the sun was bright whatever the season. Since the light was so much brighter here and not a problem, I wondered if my spirit actually had eyes. Since I did not know what I looked like, I tested it out the way I would have on earth. I squeezed my eyes shut and then opened them. Because I could feel myself doing that, I realized that in my spirit form I did have eyes. This meant that I could see things and sense that which I could not see.

Speaking of the light of God, I did not merge with the light, nor was God right before me giving off light as reported in some near-death experiences. For me, the light seemed to emanate from God in his Third Heaven and filled the entire second realm.

With regard to the first and second spiritual heavens, these two realms seemed completely separate in my observation. At creation, God separated the light from the darkness. The key word being *separated*. In these two spiritual realms, one is full of darkness (the First Heaven), the other full of light (the Second Heaven). Similarly, God separated the light from the darkness; this meant to me that the two realms had to be kept separate.

Another reason for separation is the first heavenly realm is an unsafe one where battles between the angelic powers (rebellious angels and those who honor God) are fought. It is one of darkness. Perhaps that is why, when I was in darkness on a pedestal table in the First Heaven, I was stuck to the table and could not move off it. I was safe there but would not have been if allowed to leave it. This area made up in part a kind of "tunnel" that linked the two heavens together through a portal, the only link between these two heavens I observed. It could have been alongside or at the edge of the First Heaven; I do not know. For these reasons, I interpret that the First and Second Heavens are distinctly separate.

One last word about God's light from a different perspective is, while in the Second Heaven, my spirit was enlightened over and over again with information that I lacked. On my return to earth, that enlightenment was dimmed for years because life intervened. I did not understand what much of it meant until I finally had the courage to resurrect my experience and examine it. Ultimately, it has been an incomparable blessing to me.

Shedding My Outer Armor

I stood in awe as what looked like armor began to fly off me. I was not aware that I had on any kind of armor. I do not remember being weighed down by it. The armor came off me not of my conscious doing. It reminded me of what the knights wore in the days of King Arthur and Camelot. Shedding it was a surprise and done so quickly that I could not identify the pieces as they disappeared instantly into the atmosphere. Once the armor was off, I was able to fly, totally freed from everything earthly.

Apparently, I no longer needed armor, as I was in a safe place. But what was the armor for? It was spiritual in nature, attached to my spirit as I lived in a physical body on earth. Plain and simple, armor is worn for protection. Did my spirit need protection while living in a physical, earthly body? Yes. It needed protection from evil and harmful spiritual influences and temptations. The earth realm is a realm of free will where both good and evil are allowed to operate. However, the armor was not needed here and was therefore immediately removed.

As I share later in this book, I once had a vision of an angel at the foot of my bed. The angel had on a black helmet and body armor. He was there protecting someone very special who was visiting me. For what reason would an angel need a helmet and body armor other than for protection? There is a constant war between beings of the light and beings who are not of the light. It is enough to understand that the armor on my spirit was and is necessary. I assume I have on spiritual armor right now, though I do not remember it coming back on when my spirit went back into my body.

The White Dress

Once the armor was gone, I looked down at myself to see what I had on. I was wearing a dress that was so white, it glistened. The hem radiated shards of light. The radiating light was like when, one time in winter, I walked outside on a very cold and dark evening—my eyes watered, so that when I looked up at the street light, I saw an aura around it. Rays of light shot off from the center in all directions. The dress covered all of me. I did not see my hands or feet. I exchanged the armor for a beautiful, glistening white dress.

The symbolism of wearing a white garment includes purity, sinlessness, innocence, goodness, godliness, and so forth. As beings created by God, it is not hard to imagine the Creator seeing us this way. It also signifies the contrast between our lives in physical bodies and our lives living in spirit. This reminds me of who I am as a child of God. It also reminds me that the true home of my spirit is not in a physical body in the physical earth realm, but at home with God in the spiritual realm.

Flying Above a Pastoral Scene

The angels each had a hand on my back as we flew over an earth-like setting. We came upon a pastoral scene. It was stunningly beautiful, with all the vibrancy of the colors and the peacefulness that was a part of it.

With each angel having a hand on my back, I was not flying on my own, but being guided to my expressed destination by the two of them. I could feel movement as we went through the atmosphere but felt no air flow, cold or heat, or weather at all. With them, I peacefully flew with no fear. The earthly comparison is a child walking with his parents, each one holding one of his hands as they walk with him, guiding him to where they want to go.

I do not remember flying anywhere by myself under my own power except briefly when I first saw myself in the white dress. One or both angels were always with me until we reached the Third Heaven, where I had a dirt road under my feet, but never felt the sensation of actually walking. I did, however, have the sensation of standing. I never felt my feet touching the ground or my legs moving. Everything happened so quickly there that I seemed to instantly be where I wanted to go. I only remember the sensation of lightness to my form, as when the armor came off my body and I did somersaults and flip flops in the atmosphere without falling. I then seemed able to fly, but never had the occasion to try it out again, nor did I seek it. I didn't need to. I was completely taken care of.

The Family on a Picnic and Animals in the Distance

The colors in this pastoral scene were deeply vivid and beautiful, reminiscent of the enhanced colors in a cartoon. They were colors I would have seen on the earth. I saw from some distance above the earth-like setting a family of four preparing to have a picnic. I was able to home in on them, almost like I had eagle eyes. I could tell that they were not my mother, stepfather, brother or me, although they all had brown hair like my family.

The reason why I wondered if I was viewing my family on a picnic was because they reminded me of my earthly family at a certain time in my life. The mother and children had dark brown hair, like we did. The children looked to be about 10 and 8 years old, the youngest a boy. At the time, my mother had remarried, and I remember going on picnics. We went on family picnics, yearly picnics with relatives, and those held annually by organizations they belonged to. I was curious, and that is when my eyes allowed me to see they were not my family.

I am not sure of the significance attached to why I saw a family as the focal point of this scene. Perhaps it was to acknowledge the importance of family in one's earthly life shown in an ideal world of great beauty and peace. Perhaps family is important in spiritual life as well, as demonstrated to me in my second near-death experience in Part 2 of this book.

Seeing My Soul

I was shown a globe, like a large bubble, and the angel said I was inside. I did not question him as to what he meant. I simply assumed that my soul was in the globe. I thought if I looked within it, I could see what my sins were. I could not see into the globe from the outside. From where I was standing, however, I could look through the globe to the outside. When I peered into the opening, to my surprise, it was empty.

I interpret this as being a symbol. The globe represents the earth and God's ability to see all my earthly deeds as recorded in my soul. Because it was empty, I was, in his judgment, free of sin. I remember thinking it was because Jesus died for our sins. Now, of course, I have sinned. But this indicated to me that my sins were forgiven, just as I had been taught.

Some near-death experiencers report being a ball of energy or an orb-like form of consciousness. This may be another possible interpretation of what I was seeing. A globe and an orb are similar in their overall shape. They could be a spiritual representation of a soul.

Admonished by an Angel about Good Deeds

After I looked into my soul and found no sin, I wanted to tell God about my good deeds, as I thought I was going to see him. Before I could go on, however, the angel had something to tell me about my good deeds, which he followed up immediately with a picture, or more like a vision.

"Your good deeds," he said to me, "are like filthy rags." That was startling to me! He then showed me a vision of a small squirrel that stood with the huge earth behind him. The squirrel was miniscule. I accepted what he said, as I figured he would know. Throughout my experience, when I saw my spirit, it was always small. Perhaps my good deeds equated with the size of my spirit. And I did not like being so small.

What I did not understand was how Jesus could be both a man and God, although I was taught and believed this. In my path of Christianity, I had believed that the good deeds I performed were done because I thought I should do them and take credit for them, which I now realized was the wrong motivation. Understanding the dual nature of Jesus, that he is both a man and God, and that he paid the price for my sins as the Messiah, I realized that deeds should be done in thanks to him for his gift of salvation. Done with the right and proper attitude, they are considered a fruit of salvation and acceptable to God.

It has taken many years and much study, but now I understand why the angel said my good deeds were like filthy rags. This was an extremely important point as well as a course correction to my self-centered life.

God Being All in All and an Autumn-Like Scene

When I asked the angel what the words, "God is all and in all" meant, he, in the blink of an eye, took me down to what appeared to be like the earth in this Second Heaven (at the time I thought it was the actual earth itself). I was suddenly in a wooded area during Autumn. I knew about this scripture but did not quote it accurately.

When I looked around, I noticed a bush and looked to see if there was a fire in it. Apparently, I did know about Moses and the burning bush. There was no fire in the bush.

In this part of my experience, I was admonished by the angel because I called the falling leaves "dead." His response was forceful but in a righteous way. My understanding now is that he was correcting my thinking toward God's creation. Everything is alive because God is in it, even though it may change through decay.

He also told me that Jesus is alive and has the power to hold everything together in the world. If I had any questions about how he could be both God and man, which I did, this removed them. This was another course correction for my life. Previous to this, and unbeknownst to me, I worshipped in church a powerless icon of Jesus instead of the real Jesus described to me here. His explanation was enlightening and life changing. I do not think it is a coincidence that I saw Jesus in an iconic, wooden way in a following scene.

The Lone Star in the Sky

We were so far above and away from this earth-like setting now that I could not find it in space when I looked. On earth, when we look up on a clear night, we can see the Milky Way with its many stars and planets, which is only one galaxy of many. As the angels guided me through this part of the Second Heaven, I only saw one star (although there may have been one other so distant it did not impinge much on my consciousness). I cannot imagine how vast the universe must be around our physical earth realm. I wonder about the distance between the stars. As someone who is afraid of heights, I had absolutely no fear as I was guided through the heavens. This is because I was with two angels, each with a hand on my back, who kept me safe.

Heard My Heart Beating

At this particular point, my heart began to beat so loudly that the sound filled my whole being. This reminded me that, although I was out-of-body, my body back on earth was not in a final state of death.

I will never know the answer to this question, but I wonder if it may be here, at this point back on earth, that the cardiologist who attended me had injected me with "a shot of adrenaline," as he put it. Epinephrine is the hormone adrenaline, and it is called by both names. One of the side effects is a pounding heart.

Hearing my heart beat signified to me that even though my spirit was on an incredible journey through the heavens, I was still somehow connected to my body back on earth. This is proved by the fact I ultimately returned to my body. Some near-death experiencers have reported seeing a silver cord connecting their spirit to their body, but I saw no such thing. It does not mean this was not the case with me, but that I did not see one and have no recollection of anything like that. Somehow, I was still connected. Hearing my heart beating was my connection to my physical body.

Building Blocks of Creation/The Wooden Statue of Jesus

When I saw Jesus as a carved, wooden statue as the answer to my question, I was puzzled. For me, asking about the building blocks of creation meant the same as asking if there was a primordial substance. That was the meaning behind the question I asked in my innocence and naiveté, having never read the Bible until many years later which documents the majesty of creation. Was Jesus the primordial substance? How could that be?

I have wondered about this part of my experience for such a long time. The conclusion I have come to is that since God's word has life in it, and because God himself is the essence of life, when he spoke, as in the creation process, it came forth into existence. That is the all-encompassing power and majesty of God. The angel had pointed me to Jesus, who the Bible calls the Word of God. The significance of that allusion is simply mind boggling. Jesus is the essence of God's Word and as such not only a part of the creation process but the process itself.

Whether or not there was a primordial substance in God's creation of the universe is a controversial subject among biblical scholars based on interpretation of the Hebrew text. That being said, I only know what I saw in this scene plus the biblical account which says God spoke creation into existence. My own personal belief is that there was no primordial substance. That is thinking like a human being living on Earth. I don't know anyone who has created a planet or a star. There are many people who hold patents because they have come up with something new, but they are always made out of earthly substances, never out of nothing.

Dealing with why I saw Jesus as a wooden statue has brought me to the conclusion that I did so because that is how I worshipped him in a church setting through the man-made rules of organized religion. That brought up the issue of faith versus religion. My understanding of this is that I needed to have a personal relationship with Jesus in order to understand him. That is what is meant by faith in him, which is necessary for salvation. I had been wrongly worshipping an icon.

When the angel told me that the whole world was inside Jesus, I did not question him. I simply believed him. (I discussed this above in the section, "God Being All in All and an Autumn-Like Scene" where the falling leaves were not dead but alive because God is in everything, and Jesus holds it all together.)

I asked where I was within Jesus because I was taught as a believer that I was within him. What did being in his side mean? I interpret this to mean that while on the cross to prove he was dead, a Roman soldier thrust a spear into Jesus' side, and blood and water issued forth onto the ground. Without his sacrificial death, there would have been no blood to cover our sins and, therefore, no church and no salvation. I am in his wounded side as a part of his church which began at Pentecost. And going a little farther, since God is in everything, and we are in Jesus as his church, the ultimate result is that God is in us and we are in God.

My guiding angel showed me in picture form four answers to four questions. I understood them to mean: one, God's words were used as the building blocks of creation and Jesus is the Word of God incarnate; two, I needed to worship Jesus as God and not an icon by having a personal relationship with him; three, the whole world exists within him as he holds it together; and four, the church exists because of the sacrificial death of Jesus.

During my experience in the supernatural realm, although it is hard to explain, everything the angel said to me was spoken in a way that made me think it was permanent. That was the unwavering depth of unending strength I heard in his communication to me throughout as he conveyed truths to me. It is why I believed him and never questioned what he told me or showed me. And yet, interwoven into all that was a love for God and all his creation that was innate to his being and came before everything.

I must admit that I do not have perfect understanding of this particular scene. Having read the Bible has helped in my interpretation. I do believe that my communicating angel knows it much better than I ever will. I keep finding his answers within it. Actually, that is a comfort.

Approaching the Third Heaven

As we ascended in space, we came to an overhead dome that stopped our ascent. We skimmed along under it for what seemed a short time, until we came to an opening. This is where the angels guided me in my quest to go to God.

I was curious about the dome. Its color was a dark gold, and the word "alloy" came into my mind. It was not the color of 14K, 18K or 24K gold, but darker. Also, it was of such minute thickness that I wondered if it would hold my weight.

I assumed I had form and weight, but did I? I do not know. I had only seen myself previously as a small spirit in a white dress. At that time, I was one with the dress. This is how I saw myself in the Third Heaven when I watched myself try to get past the force field. I had consciousness in this realm, like I did back on earth. My consciousness is proved by my memory of what happened during my near-death experience.

One other note of interest here is how I clearly saw that the surface of the dome was hammered in appearance. At this time, I knew nothing of the Bible's ancient understanding of the cosmos. Particularly, the Israelites believed that the earth had a solid firmament (dome) in the sky that held up waters above the dome. The Hebrew word for firmament comes from the root word *raqa* which means beat, stamp, beat out, spread out. It can refer to the process of hammering out a piece of gold (Exodus 39:3). The hammered surface I saw was a very dark gold color.

The Third Stage: Third Heaven

The Thin Metal Floor

Once I stepped foot onto the ground above the dome, I found that my weight was not a problem and didn't think anything more about it. I had no concern that this realm was supported in space by only two to three inches of thickness (which included the dirt and grass on top). To compare, the thickness to the center of the earth is approximately 3,958 miles, the mantle's thickness is 1,774 miles, and the crust's thickness is 21 miles.

Concerning my weight, I was thinking from an earthly perspective being my only means of comparison. But do our spirits have weight? Do angels have weight?

To me, from where I was standing, the terrain was similar to that of the earth. But not the sky. There was no color but grey emptiness as far as I could see or had seen on the way here through space, except for the one lone star.

A Man and Child in a Park-Like Setting

I was curious about the child because it reminded me of a snapshot of me as a young toddler. I was not sure if the child was a boy or girl because I never saw its face. The memory of that picture was what prompted the question about my biological father. I don't remember hearing the voice of the man who answered my question with a no. I don't remember if he just mouthed the word and shook his head, but think that was the case.

I was concerned because the man had left the child alone on the bench when he came to me. While I was thinking that, I noticed in my peripheral vision that an angel with open arms and a smile had immediately come to tend it. I wondered if it was because I had that thought, or if the man had already arranged it. In any event, I must have made a connection between the child (which I thought could be me) who had been left alone by the man, and my biological father leaving me alone at five years old when he died and went to heaven. I believe that connection is why I asked him if he was my father. However, it is important to remember that I had asked my two guiding angels to take me to God, my spiritual Father, and this was where they took me. My question seemed to complicate things for a moment, but he was not my father.

What stood out for me the most about the man were his eyes. They were brown and looking at me with such kindness. I could not look away. The twinkle in his eyes together with the smile on his face meant to me that he knew something about me that I did not know, but that I would like to know.

In reflection, I wonder if he knew I would eventually figure out who he was and be astonished, embarrassed, and contrite because I did not recognize who it was who met me on the path in the Third Heaven. Perhaps I should have known, but I did not. If I had, I would never have asked the question.

The encounter with this man was something I remembered years after my near-death experience. It came back to my memory while in a discussion with a family member about his baby who was soon to be born. This is when the recall emerged in my mind. So, I told him about it. He asked if I thought the man who I saw could have been Jesus. That thought had never occurred to me, so it surprised me. At some point later, during a discussion with a friend about my experience, she also thought the man I saw may have been Jesus, even though I did not mention it as a possibility. This surprised me yet again.

This man I saw was the only one who looked human throughout the whole experience. He could have been Jesus, though still I cannot say for sure. He met me on the path in the Third Heaven and seemed to know who I was, although I did not recognize him. Even so, I was allowed the next experiences that followed.

Lastly, and most peculiar, as I stood before this man, I seemed to grow a little taller in his presence. When he was whisked away, he became smaller and smaller the farther away he went, until he disappeared. I have struggled to understand this. It seemed as I grew taller, that he had instilled something intangible within me. He had given me something. But what? Logically, the bigger you are the more strength you have. Maybe he instilled strength within me. If so, for what purpose? Or perhaps it was something else? I struggle to answer these questions.

When this encounter was finished, I simply and calmly accepted what I had seen. I turned and looked down the road to continue my journey. And what I saw next excited me and made me happy.

The Entrance to God's Dwelling Place/City

In this pastoral scene, I had come to the end of the road, literally. A deep chasm was in front of me. I looked to see if Abraham was in it. I was aware of the story of Abraham's bosom as referring to the place where the righteous Israelites went when they died. He was not there, as the righteous dead were there only until Jesus' resurrection.

On the other side of the chasm, a cloud obscured what must have been a house, since only one room was visible outside the cloud. I understood that God's heavenly city/domain was either within the cloud or behind it. What I could see of the room was surrounded by what turned out to be a force field.

The chasm sloped downward off to my left. The angel told me I needed to jump over it and not fall into it. I wondered if it was an entry point leading down to somewhere I did not want to go, perhaps even Hades. I thought that if I fell into it, I might never get out. Nevertheless, I was confident I could jump over it and was not fearful.

My Small Spirit

On trying to get back over the chasm, instead of myself, I saw my small spirit jump over the chasm on the third try and watched while it did. I (my consciousness) was watching my small spirit (who was what I looked like in the Second Heaven) jump over the chasm, as it seemed to split away from my consciousness. I was totally aware of where I stood. I did not know what kind of appearance I had while watching my small spirit (perhaps the globe/orb with eyes in it that I saw upon looking back over the chasm?). I sensed I had some sort of form because I was very much aware of standing and watching what was happening during these moments.

My small spirit came back into me when I/it could not gain entrance into what I understood was God's house, and the only room I was allowed to see. I wanted to and tried three times because I knew where I came from and where I belonged. My real home is with God, my creator. And when I was rejected, my small spirit bounced right back into me in the spot where, if I had been in human form, would have been between my ribs. I never saw its face. Its back was to me when it jumped, and when it returned and reentered me. I neither felt nor expected it.

From my experience, it seems that our consciousness is our spiritual being (some call this spirit, some soul). I have tried to understand our spiritual nature because it never occurred to me that a split, or a fracturing off of my spirit from my consciousness, could occur. My faculties remained with my consciousness, but I became two separate entities. This did not upset me. I simply watched my small spirit as it did what I would have done. This all largely remains a great mystery to me.

Looking into a Room

The room looked like a flower conservatory. The flowers, however, looked like they were carved out of wood. They were all of the same variety but had different colored petals and centers. I interpreted that the flowers represented people gathered together in a church listening to God's word, symbolized by the rain, but not absorbing its instruction to obtain blessings. Now why is that? Perhaps I was like that. Perhaps that was the message for me. Following religious practices by rote will not get me into heaven. That is a relationship with the ritualistic church. Christianity is a relationship with God and his son, and not a religion. I do not think it matters in what particular denomination or church you find this, if any, so long as that relationship is paramount. This was another of life's course corrections that I received.

Heart Pounding Loudly

At this point, I heard my heart pounding loudly for the second and last time during my experience. It reminded me again that my body back on earth was not fully dead. This happened just before entering the room protruding from the cloud that obscured whatever was behind it. I interpret this as needing to hear my heartbeat because I was not going to enter into the room. I was not going to see God the Father at this time because I was not fully dead and past the point of no return. The guiding angel did say I was not expected, which likely meant it was not my time.

Another reason why I heard my heart beating so loudly could be if I was given another shot of adrenaline at this point on earth. However, I do not know if this was the case.

Not Allowed to Enter

It is obvious to all that in order to enter into and remain in the eternal heavenly city, one must be deceased. Since it was not my time to die, I was not allowed to enter. However, it was a blessing for me to actually come right up to it. I was given a very important message from the contents of that room. It is a sort of summary of the whole experience. I could not find my way to the truth of God through my current church. I had to find it elsewhere.

On another note, being that close means that I was very close to fully dying, due to the severity of the reaction I had to the allergy injection. The final result was that I was given more time to make the course corrections I had been given, for which I am eternally thankful to God my Father for his kindness and mercy toward me.

The Fenced Field and Wind

A strong wind abruptly turned me around, and I now faced the road from where I had entered. Obviously, it was time to leave, and in a hurry. Why in a hurry? Perhaps my bodily functions on earth were about to come back to normal, and the precise time had come to return to it. On a side note, in the Bible, the Holy Spirit is sometimes symbolized by the wind. Perhaps it was the Holy Spirit rushing me out to meet that precise timeline.

Speaking of wind, as time went on during my lifetime, I remember being rather anxious when the wind was strongly gusting outside and hoping it would do no damage. I still feel that way, and if it is really windy outside, I will opt to stay inside. I never attributed it to this experience, but it could be linked. I could no more have stopped myself from moving forward even if I had wanted to on my way to exit this realm.

As I went along the road, three angels on each side of me were protecting my spirit. When we came to the white fenced-in area, I took a quick look around it while propelled forward by the wind at my back. I interpret the green bushes as representing life. In contrast, the sparse brown grass and the tree with a few brown leaves on it represented death. This could symbolize the difference between good and evil. Since some branches on the green bushes were laying on the fence, that makes me wonder if, symbolically, I was "on the fence" in my Christian walk. Good, evil, and on the fence seemed to be choices. Taken together as a whole, the Bible teaches that people, like trees, should bear fruit. There was no fruit on that tree. The field itself may have represented the state of my spiritual life at that time. It was time to get off the fence and bear some fruit. That was the message I took from this scene.

Park-Like Setting

We were nearing the exit where I saw the park-like setting when I had first entered this realm. I looked to see if I could find the man I had seen, the one who had interacted briefly with me, but I did not see him. I noticed that the bench he sat on with the child on his lap also was not there. There was nothing for me to see here but a park. I was disappointed not to find him still there. Interestingly, the disappointment had no emotion attached to it, perhaps because I did not know who he was.

In the spiritual dimension, I could feel negative feelings like disappointment or apprehension but without negative emotion attached to it. In other words, I was disappointed, but it was okay. On the other hand, I experienced the positive feelings of happiness and joy, like I would have on earth. It seems in that realm there is an absence of fear. There was no fear behind the disappointment, or apprehension, or the chastisement, or even the mocking laughter I would experience next. I accepted it all as fact, like I did with every aspect of my near-death experience.

Mocking Laughter

On the way out, as I was rushed toward the Third Heaven's exit, I heard mocking laughter coming from the sky above the fenced-in area. I interpret this as coming from some sort of maleficent spirit. It gladly laughed at me because I had been denied entrance into God's house after repeated tries. This spirit liked that I did not get in and was being hurried to the exit. I did not like that he was laughing at me; however, I gave it no more thought. My only consolation here is that I was not dead. It is not like I died and was barred entry.

Perhaps this was the reason I needed an escort of angels to accompany me to the exit. They were a protective force. They were also waiting for me on earth, also in protective mode. The lesson I take from all this is not to entertain evil in any way, shape or form. I saw how that evil spirit behaved toward me, and its behavior was reprehensible. I learned it is always best to remove one's self from the darkness of evil because it mocks God's goodness. God meant it for good to send me back to earth to accomplish his will for my life.

Sent Back Down

One of the six angels awaited me at the exit site. The other angels were gone, and so were my two guiding angels. We were alone at the exit. I had not seen my main guiding angel, who had communicated with me throughout the experience, since the time he asked if I could jump over the chasm.

I wish I could describe this angel at the exit, but I cannot. I only remember that the angel gestured toward the sheet and seemed to encourage me to get on the slide back to earth. I was apprehensive. There was a grey, empty, outer space in front of and surrounding it.

Thinking about it now, it would be like sliding down through the cosmos—a scary proposition. However, before I knew it, I jumped on the sheet without a thought. I have no recollection of the descent. It must have been instantaneous, like all the places where I immediately found myself when my guiding angel took me to them. I was now back on earth and still in my spiritual body.

The Fourth Stage: Back to Earth

The Landing

As I returned to earth after the descent from the Third Heaven, I slipped off the slide to the floor in the back hallway of my doctor's office. One moment I was on the sheet-slide, and the next moment I was on the earth. I felt love all around me. Both my guiding angels who had been with me from the beginning were waiting for me. One was guarding me from behind, and I sensed his wings were open but did not see them. The other angel was crouched down in front of me at eye level. Throughout my experience, he stood beside me as he took me from one place to another. For this one time only, we were face to face. Even so, I do not remember what his face looked like, or anything else about him except that he was there. And I had questions to ask him.

Speaking with the Angel

I asked the angel if my doctor would be held responsible for what he had done to me. His answer surprised and perplexed me. His exact words were, "No, he will not be held responsible, he will be held accountable." There is a big difference between "responsible" and "accountable." After many years, I have come to the inevitable conclusion that this was another life course correction for me.

To say the least, I did not like his answer. What I learned, however, was that I am accountable to God for what I do with my own body, which includes what I do to others, and my intentions. In hindsight, I had put my faith in my doctor's expertise and trusted in his ability. I believed then and now that he was trying to help and meant no harm. He did not know that I would respond in such a life-threatening way, and hence, why the angel said that he would not be held responsible. But accountable, yes, to sift out his intentions in it all. Unsurprisingly, now I ask a lot of questions before I commit to any doctor's recommendations. I am accountable to God and responsible for myself.

I also asked the angel, "What am I supposed to do with my life? I never want my spirit to be that small again." At this point, I may have been standing because it seemed now that he was in front of a wall with a short barrier of some sort in front of him but still in a sort of crouched position. And now he held an open book in his hand. I did not notice the book until I asked the question. The book was thick, had a black cover, and was open about two-thirds to the back. He was looking at the words intently and somewhat absorbed, but then he looked up at me.

At this moment, I became distracted. I sensed activity swirling around me and looked around. Suddenly, I was pulled like a magnet toward my body, which I could see through the open door at the end of the hallway to my left. Something like radio static filled the air. When I looked back at the angel while being pulled toward my body, which I could not control, my last thought was about the open book he held in his hand. Was I to start a book club? Write a book? Read a book? I could not hear his answer through what seemed like chaos swirling around me.

When I first saw him holding the book, I wondered if it was the Book of Life. For some reason, I decided it was not. Looking back, if it was the Book of Life, my name was already in it since I had just visited the Third Heaven. But now, so many years later, I understand that there is another book where our deeds are written from birth to death. But I was 26 years old at this time, the book was a thick one, and I know what the angel thought of my good deeds. Are our deeds written in a book housed in eternity before we even do them? Does God know the paths of our lives from beginning to end and the experiences we will have? Both the Bible and near-death experience research data suggest that each person's deeds are recorded. Is that what the angel was reading about? I am just not sure what this book was exactly, but it does make sense that it could likely be some sort of book of deeds, either past, present, and/or future.

In any event, at that time and for the vast majority of my life, I interpreted the book as having been the Bible. I interpreted my whole experience as pointing to the Bible—mainly because that was where I was so deficient, and why I needed the life lessons. If I were to walk the Christian path, I needed to conform my thinking to the Bible. After I read the Bible, it made a big difference going forward.

This was the last time I saw this precious angel who had helped me through my unexpected adventure through the three heavens. I am forever grateful to God that he sent the two of them to guide me, correct me, and keep me safe. I cannot come up with adequate words to express the enormity of my gratitude. I suppose it would take an eternity. I never thought anything like this could ever happen to me or anyone for that matter, and still find it hard to believe.

The Hallway of Angels

Six angels lined the hallway that led straight to my human body. They appeared to be the same ones who had escorted me to the Third Heaven's exit. I wondered where they had gone. It seems the reason why was to go before me to prepare for my reentry and safe return to my human body. They were there when I landed in the hallway. They were part of the love I felt surrounding me. Three angels stood on each side of the hallway with their faces toward the wall. Their wings seemed brown in color and were spread out touching each other like a protective barrier. They were standing a few feet off the ground. All were attired in a long gown, very light in color, almost white. As far as their height, in comparison to me, my guess is that they were a little shorter than six feet tall. For some reason they seemed female, but I cannot attest to that. They protected my spirit as it whooshed through the hallway to my body. This was the last time I saw them. I am forever grateful to God for all their help, and the love I felt from them.

But from what, exactly, were they protecting me? This is a similar question as to why my spirit had on armor until I reached the Second Heaven. Also, it is similar to why, in the vision of my unborn child, he had a protecting angel in full armor with him (see Chapter 11). All I can say is there must be some kind of spiritual battle ever waging. God does not leave his spiritual children unprotected in the spiritual or earthly realms. The angels protected my spirit until my spirit and body became one. Perhaps they put my spiritual armor back on, which had been removed in the Second Heaven.

My Spirit Moving Back into My Body

It was now time for my spirit to reenter my human body. I was in the room standing next to the gurney where my body lay inert. At this point, I do not remember hearing any static. The pulling away was similar to how I saw the man in the Third Heaven get whisked away.

As I stood alongside the gurney, I knew that body was mine without question. Whether the body somehow recognized its spirit and pulled it to where it lay, or we recognized each other, I do not know. I had left it on a gurney, and now I was returning to it on a gurney. My body was not in the same room where I had left it, however. The room was smaller. My body was not positioned as I had left it, opposite the door and alongside the wall. It was now positioned with its feet toward the door and was in the middle of the room.

I next was a few inches above my inert form through no effort of my own. I do not remember if it was covered with a blanket or not. My understanding later on was that the doctor had covered and uncovered me as the effects of the adrenaline wore off.

It never once occurred to me that my spirit could not or would not fit into my body. I also did not sense that it went outside its limits. I squirmed down from those few inches above my form until I reached it or came very near to it, I do not know, as I did not control this process. My spirit seemed to know exactly what to do and so did my body. My body softly absorbed my spirit and the reconnection was complete. I felt nothing.

My consciousness was there and aware throughout the process of reconnection and also after. I did not suddenly awake. It was my body that awoke upon its spirit's entry. I was conscious of the process and knew when it had ended. As it did, I realized I was back, and my first thought was that I could no longer hear my heart pounding, which was a relief. My second thought was to make sure my extremities were in working order. I lifted my arms and legs one at a time. When I was satisfied that they were working, and I expected them to, I was amused that I had tested them. I was a human being again: body, soul and spirit. However, I did not feel well. I felt ill. And that was when the doctor walked into my room. There was no more time to figure everything out.

My understanding is that the spirit itself never really becomes a part of the physical earthly realm, although it somehow interacts with it and is connected to it via the body. The spirit enmeshes with the physical body. When it leaves, it takes with it all the body's consciousness, its mind and memories. At least, that is how it seemed to me. This is what makes each spirit unique. It is the spirit's essence and it can be identified somehow in that way. Its return to the body wakes up the body, and one's humanity immediately returns, as it did with me.

Looking at things this way is logical to me because I returned to my human body as the same person who left it—the exception, of course, is that now I had a supernatural experience as a part of my conscious memory.

4

Scriptural Connections

Because I had not read the Bible at the time of my near-death experience, I was mostly ignorant of any kind of biblical description relating to almost all the parts of my experience. It was not until years later that I opened the Bible and read it through. I was amazed to find scriptures that were relevant to the lessons I was taught. I will share those that helped me make connections to what occurred. They also add to the authenticity of the experience.

The Pedestal Table

The Bible references the area where battles are fought in the first heavenly spiritual realm between the faithful and unfaithful angels:

"But the prince of the Persian kingdom resisted me twenty-one days. Then Michael, one of the chief princes, came to help me because I was detained there with the King of Persia." (Daniel 10:13 NIV)

The Light

In our physical earth realm, the brightest light in the sky is the sun. We are never to look straight at it or we could become blind. When Moses asked to see God's glory, God said to him:

"You cannot see my face, for man shall not see me and live." (Exodus 33:20)

Shedding My Armor

"Put on the whole armor of God that you may be able to stand against the schemes of the devil." (Ephesians 6:11)

"Stand therefore, having fastened on the belt of truth, and having put on the breastplate of righteousness, and, as shoes for your feet, having put on the readiness given by the gospel of peace. In all circumstances take up the shield of faith, with which you can extinguish all the flaming darts of the evil one; and take the helmet of salvation, and the sword of the Spirit, which is the word of God." (Ephesians 6:14-17)

The White Dress

"The one who conquers will be clothed thus in white garments, and I will never blot his name out of the book of life. I will confess his name before my Father and before his angels." (Revelation 3:5)

"And his clothes became radiant, intensely white, as no one on earth could bleach them." (Mark 9:3)

The Family on a Picnic and Animals in the Distance

God said to Adam and Eve:

"And God blessed them. And God said to them, 'Be fruitful and multiply and fill the earth and subdue it, and have dominion over the fish of the sea and over the birds of the heavens and over every living thing that moves on the earth.'" (Genesis 1:28)

God said to Noah and his sons after the flood:

"And you, be fruitful and multiply, increase greatly on the earth and multiply in it." (Genesis 9:7)

Seeing My Soul

"For all have sinned and fall short of the glory of God." (Romans 3:23)

"Who gave himself for our sins to deliver us from the present evil age, according to the will of our God and Father." (Galatians 1:4)

"For the wages of sin is death, but the free gift of God is eternal life in Christ Jesus our Lord." (Romans 6:23)

Admonished by an Angel about Good Deeds

"All of us have become like one who is unclean, and all our righteous acts are like filthy rags; we all shrivel up like a leaf, and like the wind our sins sweep us away." (Isaiah 64:6 NIV)

God Being All in All and an Autumn-Like Scene

"One God and Father of all, who is over all and through all and in all." (Ephesians 4:6)

"And Moses said, 'I will turn aside to see this great sight, why the bush is not burned.'" (Exodus 3:3)

"'Putting everything in subjection under [Jesus's] feet.' Now in putting everything in subjection to him, he left nothing outside his control. At present, we do not yet see everything in subjection to him." (Hebrews 2:8)

"You shall not make for yourself a carved image, or any likeness of anything that is in heaven above, or that is in the earth beneath, or that is in the water under the earth." (Exodus 20:4)

The Lone Star in the Sky

"Is not God high in the heavens? See the highest stars, how lofty they are!" (Job 22:12)

This scripture spoke to me because, although I am afraid of heights, I was never afraid when I flew through the heavens with the angels:

"Jesus looked at them and said, 'With man it is impossible, but not with God. For all things are possible with God.'" (Mark 10:27)

The Building Blocks of Creation/The Wooden Statue of Jesus

"In the beginning, God created the heavens and the earth. The earth was without form and void, and darkness was over the face of the deep. And the Spirit of God was hovering over the face of the waters. And God said, 'Let there be light,' and there was light."
(Genesis 1:1-3)

In the following scripture, John speaks about Jesus:

"In the beginning was the Word, and the Word was with God, and the Word was God. He was in the beginning with God. All things were made through him, and without him was not any thing made that was made. In him was life, and the life was the light of men." (John 1:1-3)

"'You have crowned [Jesus] with glory and honor, putting everything in subjection under his feet.' Now in putting everything in subjection to him, he left nothing outside his control. At present, we do not yet see everything in subjection to him." (Hebrews 2:7-8)

"[Jesus] is the radiance of the glory of God and the exact imprint of his nature, and he upholds the universe by the word of his power." (Hebrews 1:3)

"'For my thoughts are not your thoughts, neither are your ways my ways,' declares the Lord. 'For as the heavens are higher than the earth, so are my ways higher than your ways and my thoughts than your thoughts.'" (Isaiah 55:8-9)

"Yet for us there is one God, the Father, from whom are all things and for whom we exist, and one Lord, Jesus Christ, through whom are all things and through whom we exist." (1 Corinthians 8:6)

"Whoever confesses that Jesus is the Son of God, God abides in him, and he in God." (1 John 4:15)

"Now faith is the assurance of things hoped for, the conviction of things not seen." (Hebrews 11:1)

"But one of the soldiers pierced his side with a spear, and at once there came out blood and water." (John 19:34)

A Man and Child in a Park-Like Setting

"But Jesus called them to him, saying, "Let the children come to me, and do not hinder them, for to such belongs the kingdom of God." (Luke 18:16)

"Jesus said to him, 'I am the way, and the truth, and the life. No one comes to the Father except through me.'" (John 14:16)

The Entrance to God's Dwelling Place/City

"And in Hades, being in torment, he lifted up his eyes and saw Abraham far off and Lazarus at his side." (Luke 16:23)

The Fenced Field and Wind

"And suddenly there came from heaven a sound like a mighty rushing wind, and it filled the entire house where they were sitting." (Acts 2:2)

"So as to walk in a manner worthy of the Lord, fully pleasing to him: bearing fruit in every good work and increasing in the knowledge of God." (Colossians 1:10)

Part 2

My Second Near-Death Experience

5

TO A COUNCIL AND BACK

It was the weekend, and the family was at home. My husband was puttering around in his workshop. My two young sons were playing together indoors. My preteen daughter was in her room. The year was 1975.

I was not feeling well and went upstairs to my bedroom to rest. As I approached my bed, I started feeling pain in my abdomen. Lying down did not help, so I got up and walked into the bathroom. The pain increased in intensity quickly, to the point where I could not stand it. It became excruciating. I began moaning. I prayed to God and asked him to take me, just before I fainted.

The very next moment, I was standing out in space. But this lasted only for an instant. Immediately in the next instant, I was now standing on a thin, clear surface (some kind of floor) looking through a window into a large room. The room was like a corporate boardroom filled with a number of people. My impression was that a meeting had just adjourned, as some in attendance were walking to the door, some were standing in small groups, some still sitting, and some getting up from their chairs.

I looked around the room to see if I recognized anyone, but I did not. One person, however, a woman, was looking at me so intently that she caught my eye. She was standing at the far end of the room, directly opposite but a little below me, behind the table and against the wall. The door to the room was off to her right. She looked at me with recognition and expectation on her face, but I did not know who she was. For a moment, a thought occurred to me that she could be my maternal grandmother, but I decided she was too young. She looked to be in her 20s or 30s. She had on a long, light-colored dress. She had brown hair and eyes. She seemed disappointed when she realized I did not recognize her. She lowered her eyes and turned her head to the left for a moment as if listening to someone tell her information about me. Then, she looked back at me with a twinkle in her eye and a half-smile that lit up her face. It was as if she had just heard something pleasant or happy about me that I did not know, that may have concerned our ancestors.

At that moment, a man walked through a door to her left. I had not noticed the door before. He politely acknowledged her by a slight nod of his head. He had an aura of importance about him. I watched as he turned quickly and began to walk alongside the wall in my direction, until I lost sight of him from my vantage point. All of a sudden, the man loomed up in front of the window. His upper body and outstretched arms blotted the room out of my sight.

The man was then outside the room and standing beside me on the clear surface. For some reason, I wondered if he had chaired the meeting. He did not speak, but he communicated telepathically to my mind. He gestured toward the window and said the people in the room were my relatives. He then added that this was one of God's councils. I wondered, although he did not include himself, if he also was a relative. I asked him if he was my father (who had died when I was five), but he became flustered and taken aback that I would ask him such a question—he did a full body pout in dismay. After this, he turned his head to the left for a moment, as if listening in the same way the woman did previously. He then turned calmly back to me and said, "No."

I wish I could describe him, but I really can't. I can say that he did not look like any of the angels I had seen in my first near-death experience and subsequent experiences. My impression is he was not an angel. Something about him made me think he was an older, ancient being. I wondered if he was the go-between appointed to convey the council's decision of my relatives to God, and then God's decision to me.

He went on to tell me that the council had made the decision that it was not my time to die, and that I still had work to do. Then he extended a finger pointing to a spot over my right shoulder. I turned and looked into outer space where he pointed. I saw what looked like a hand-drawn wavy line of two mountains connected by a valley in the immense grey expanse. He said, "The first mountain is your husband," and called him by name. He then said, "The second is like unto it." He then extended his arm, opened his hand, palm up, and dismissed me. I looked back at him as my spirit immediately left him. The next thing I knew, I was back on earth in my body.

I regained consciousness in the bathroom where I had left. The pain was gone. My husband was kneeling beside me, and two little wide-eyed boys were peeking around the door at us. Once they realized I was all right, they went back to whatever they were doing. My husband said that our daughter had heard me moaning, and when she found me unconscious, she alerted him. She was in her room crying. After walking me back to bed, he went to check on her. The crisis was thankfully over. The cause was an allergic reaction to an ingredient in something I had eaten.

6

INTEGRATION

When I came back to earthly consciousness, I was relieved to be free from the pain and to have my life back. I did not really think the first mountain, which symbolized my husband, was anything to be concerned about. However, the second mountain symbolized an unknown person, and so I would have to wait and see who it turned out to be. Having made that decision, the vision of the two mountains receded into the background of my life.

During the first few weeks afterward, I was more upset about my body's reaction to the allergic substance than about the near-death experience that had ensued. It surprised me. I never thought in a million years that something like that would happen to me again. But at least this time I knew what it was. Even so, I had to move on with my life. I had young children to care for, so I occupied myself with family and the life around me, and thought no more about it.

I did not tell anyone about this experience right after I had it, not even my husband. My immediate family knew that I had fainted and recovered, and that was all they needed to know. I did not want to worry any of them. As far as others were concerned, my allergies were my personal business. And as far as the near-death experience was concerned, who would believe it? They would probably think I was crazy or delusional. I thought it best to keep it to myself, like I did my other spiritual encounters.

Integration

Over the next period of years, my husband and I raised our family. I cannot think of a time I thought about this near-death experience. But it came up again from the recesses of my memory one Christmas many years later.

At the time it resurfaced, my children were grown and gone from home, and my husband was recently deceased. I was alone. I was given a Christmas gift, a tin of nuts, all of one variety. The nuts were enhanced with various flavors and divided into sections according to flavor. I ate a few nuts each day for two or three days, when all of a sudden, I had an unexpected allergic reaction. It was not a severe one, but it alarmed me nonetheless. It reminded me of the near-death experience I had about 26 years prior. The pain that precipitated that experience was one I never wanted to encounter again. I stopped eating the nuts and called a specialist for an appointment.

On recalling the near-death experience, I remembered the drawing of the two mountains connected by a valley. With my husband's death, the first part of the vision had been fulfilled and was now no longer relevant. I considered him a man of God and did not think he needed any help from me on that score. I was meant to help him, especially with emotional support, during the last ten years of his life while his health deteriorated. I did it willingly and out of love and respect for him.

The second mountain symbolizing an unknown person had not yet come to fruition. Since that was the case, I tucked the memory away again. Now, many years later, the memory resurfaced because I finally came to understand who the second mountain symbolized. It was time to fulfill my God-given assignment. It took 45 years from the near-death experience to identify this mystery person.

At this point, the near-death experience and its vision were front and center. The "like unto it" person was now finally revealed. With this knowledge, I try to be an emotional support for this person on the physical side and an example on the spiritual side. I am determined to do what I can for as long as I can.

When the man in my near-death experience long ago told me the meaning of the vision, I understood and accepted it. The decision had been made and there was no changing it. I was not given a choice to stay or leave. And back in my body, all earthly things presented themselves.

It is a common theme in near-death experience accounts for people to be sent back after having been told they still "have work to do." In my first near-death experience, the angel said to me at the outset that I was not expected. That meant it was not my time to die. As for this second near-death experience, it was not my time, either. While in the heavenly realm, through God's grace, the man granted me certain important knowledge. He explained the vision shown to me, or I never would have understood its meaning. I am most grateful to him for that.

I have not been told of any other specific work assigned at this particular time other than what was told during my two near-death experiences. Together, they have impacted most of my life. But, generally speaking, there is always work to be done, both on the spiritual side and on the human side. It never ends until death. Time marches on, and we need to run the race to the finish line as best we can to where our eternal destiny awaits.

7

INTERPRETATIONS, EXPLANATIONS AND LESSONS

Similar to my first near-death experience, I had many questions remaining afterward. However, it was not until many years later that I turned my full attention to understanding what I experienced. Despite its brevity, this experience brought deep mystery and very special meaning.

Asking God to Take Me

The background leading up to this second near-death experience includes certain spiritual events that had occurred: my first near-death experience before I was married; seeing a golden glow around my neighbor's deceased body; a vision of my unborn son; and a dream that heaven was closing its door, and I barely made it through before it slammed shut.

Having had previous spiritual experiences, I was desperate to be free of the terrible pain. We all have a certain threshold for pain. I had reached mine and exceeded it. The pain was too much for me to handle or overcome. The only way I knew how to end it was to ask God to take me. In God's doing so, I learned unequivocally that he does answer prayers. I trust he will do it in his way, which is best for us and to his glory.

Leaving My Body

I did not feel myself leave my body. I did not fly up through the heavens as in my first near-death experience. No angels assisted me or guarded me this time. It was an instantaneous transition from my physical self to my spiritual self, from my home on earth to standing on a clear surface in front of a window in heaven, and from unbearable pain to no pain. I forgot all about the pain as I focused my attention on the activity going on in the room.

The Thin, Clear Surface

I was standing in outer space in front of the window of a tall building under a light grey sky. Empty space was everywhere I looked. I wondered how this was possible. Immediately, a thin, clear surface, like a see-through platform, appeared beneath me. It was shaped like a sidewalk and was attached to the building for several feet. It then made a 90-degree angle for another several feet facing the emptiness of space.

Now feeling more secure, and with that distraction behind me, I directed my attention to the window and peered in. The window itself was in the upper portion of the room so that I looked down slightly on those who were inside. No one in the room noticed me except for one woman.

The Woman

If any of my known deceased relatives were in the room, I did not recognize them. I wondered if the woman I saw could be my maternal grandmother. She was petite with dark brown hair and eyes, as my grandmother would have looked when she was young. That was my original thought, but I discarded it because she appeared as a young woman.

I could tell the woman was disappointed that I did not recognize her. I only wish I knew what she heard when she turned her head to the left and then back to me and smiled with what looked like approval, all disappointment leaving her face.

It is interesting to note that the three beings I saw who looked human all interacted with me: the woman here, and the man when I entered the Third Heaven in my first near-death experience, and the man in this experience. Also, they all turned their heads to the left as if listening to someone and then turned back to me (two with a smile, and one without one). The man who communicated with me in this experience was the one who did not smile at me.

The Man

The spiritual being who looked like a man communicated with me from his mind to mine, and I communicated from my mind to his. The two angels in my first near-death experience and the other angels I write about later in this book communicated with me telepathically as well.

The man had walked through a doorway that was next to the young woman who had caught my attention. He had an aura of importance about him. I wondered who he was. Had he chaired the meeting? Perhaps he was serving as some kind of council overseer. Regardless of his function, people were leaving the room. That confused me because, before I lost sight of him, he spoke to no one as he walked in my direction toward the back of the room.

When someone popped up in the window, I thought it was this same being. It would only have taken him a few seconds to get there. Then he was standing next to me on the see-through platform. He explained what I had been looking at. Both the fact that they were my relatives and one of God's councils was a surprise to me. I had never heard that there were any other councils but the one written in Psalm 82. Because of my past experience, I knew that things often worked instantaneously in the spirit world. The council members knew their decision had been approved and that is why they were leaving before the man even came through the door. Their job was done. It was apparent that this man had been appointed to communicate their decision to me.

Concerning his appearance, he seemed to be older than any spiritual being I had ever seen. I was curious about him and sensed at the time that he may have been an ancient being. He was a little taller than me. I cannot remember his apparel when he stood next to me. More than anything, I was interested in hearing what he had to say to me.

His look of utter astonishment and incredulousness when I asked him if he was my father is something I can never forget. My memory of this moment is vivid. The pout he did in frustration at my question is also something that remains surprising to me.

The only reason I can come up with in regard to asking the question was the fact that this was a council meeting of my relatives, and I did not know what his function had been in that meeting, if any. Was he one of my relatives, too? That probably sparked the memory of my father. I was in heaven and was told when I was five years old that heaven is where my father was taken when he died. The inner child in me still missed him.

The feeling of calmness the man exuded when he turned back to me is equally as vivid. It was as if I had never asked the question. I was still reeling from his reaction, not understanding how he had so quickly moved on and with no explanation. I am grateful that God sent him to me for his explanation of the vision. Without it, I don't think I would ever have understood the symbolic meaning of the drawing in the ether. It is something of a miracle to be told what was expected of me in my future on earth.

This was the second time I had asked a being who looked like a man, and not an angel, if he was my father. I have learned not to ask that question.

Interpretations, Explanations and Lessons

The Council

A question that remains unanswered for me concerns my relatives and the council. The Bible pictures God in his council (Psalm 82; 1 Kings 22:19-22) where he holds judgment. But, as in my case, do other heavenly councils exist? Are there councils of relatives involved in decision-making processes for those alive on the earth who have near-death experiences? Do they make recommendations to God who then makes the final decision? Or are they autonomous and their decisions stand? I cannot imagine that God's approval was unnecessary. For that reason, I considered that the spirit communicating with me could have been a go-between from my council of relatives to God and then to me.

I saw perhaps 20 to 30 people in the room. The one thing I do not know is how many people had already left the meeting before I looked through the window. But who were they? Were they my father's side of the family or my mother's? Or both? That would have made them my ancestors, that is, those in my direct lineage by blood. But he did not say that. He said they were my relatives. Relatives are those in the same family connected by blood, marriage or adoption. That would include my ancestors, in-laws, and their wider families. Another question then is were they chosen or had they volunteered? I could go on asking questions, but it remains a mystery as to who specifically they were, and one I cannot solve.

The Council's Decision

The council rendered a judgment concerning my request for God to take me. My request was denied. God answered my prayer and showed me the seriousness of the request by placing it before a council. The life he gives us is precious in his sight.

I believe that, because God is omniscient, he knows when we will be born and when we will die. Just because he knows this does not mean he causes it. Since that is the case, I believe when God assigns us something to do for him it is at some point within the timeframe of birth and death, and is for our good and his glory. I came to this philosophy many years ago while pondering my father's death, and it made me feel better about it. I trust my father had completed whatever task God had assigned him. He was not taken away from me because God needed him, as I was told and believed at the time. That, however, does not mean I did not miss him as an adult and wonder from time to time what our family life would have been like if he had lived longer.

My council of relatives sent me back to earth to complete my assigned task. This is what the man explained to me, and what this near-death experience was all about.

A remaining question is how could the council make any decision about me? They would have had to know all about my life, including the future. Perhaps they had access to my personal book of deeds and were privileged to read it. If so, I had not come to the end of what had been written about me. Did they have the power to change my life's ending? Whether or not they did, it must have been more important for me to complete my earthly, God-given job than to stay in heaven. I accepted their decision with no question.

People wonder what they are going to do in heaven. Perhaps being a member of a council of relatives is an example of one job. Apparently, just like we have jobs on earth, so too will we have work to do in the spiritual realm.

My work on earth was not yet completed, and to me that meant my spiritual work in the earthly realm was not finished. It is sometimes hard to come up with an answer to the question of what is our purpose on earth. At this time, however, to my utter amazement, I was actually told. The word amazement does not quite cover the immensity of that knowledge. Although the spirit showed me in symbolic form and decoded it in just a few words, it was now up to me to do it.

Interpretations, Explanations and Lessons

Some near-death experiencers report being told they must return to earth even if they prefer not to, and are kindly told why. I was simply told I still had work to do, and what it was. I was then summarily dismissed and instantaneously back in my body, exactly where I had left it. This was so unlike my first near-death experience where I asked what I was to do with my life but was not able to hear the answer. However, on looking back, the answer was already given within the experience, I just did not realize it at the time. Both near-death experiences addressed timely issues of importance to be implemented going forward in my life.

The Two Mountains

After the man told me the council's decision, he explained what the two mountains that had been drawn in the atmosphere represented. I did not see him draw the mountains, if he did. I only saw them when he pointed them out to me. The drawing was like a vision in the sky.

The man used my husband's first name as the person representing the first mountain. I do not know why, but using his name surprised me. As his wife, I was his helpmate, so that was not a surprise. I found it unusual, though, that apparently there is nothing hidden about us in the spiritual realm. The "like unto it" person the second mountain represented was not revealed to me. The mountains were connected by a valley. At the time, I did not know if this was significant, nor did I understand the significance of the wording "like unto it," which also could have meant anything. This would not all become clear for many years.

As you get older, there comes a time when you must make peace with yourself. It is like straightening the house so everything is in its place, or like righting a wrong. It is a feeling of satisfaction, of getting everything done. Many years after the second near-death experience, I began to wonder again who the second mountain symbolized. I was getting older and had still not identified the mystery person. Once you have a near-death experience, it is not something you can forget. It is always with you even if locked away, and it surfaces on its own when something innocently said or done unlocks it from your hiding place.

And then, sure enough, the second part of the prophetic vision I saw in heaven came true. The mystery was finally solved. I connected all the dots. It had taken 45 years. Everything fit so perfectly that I could not deny it. By God's grace, I am currently in the process of doing my best to do whatever necessary to satisfactorily complete my God-given "work" with the sensitivity and love that I think God would expect.

My hope is that at the end of my life I can say the same thing to God that Paul said to King Agrippa about his mission while on the earth: "O King Agrippa, I was not disobedient to the heavenly vision" (Acts 26:19).

8

SCRIPTURAL CONNECTIONS

As with my first near-death experience, I will share scriptures that helped me make connections to what occurred. They add to the authenticity of the experience.

The Council

The Bible pictures God as ruling in his council in the following two scriptures:

"God has taken his place in the divine council; in the midst of the gods he holds judgment." (Psalm 82:1)

"And Micaiah said, 'Therefore hear the word of the Lord: I saw the Lord sitting on his throne, and all the host of heaven standing beside him on his right hand and on his left; and the Lord said, "Who will entice Ahab, that he may go up and fall at Ramoth-gilead?" And one said one thing, and another said another. Then a spirit came forward and stood before the Lord, saying, "I will entice him." And the Lord said to him, "By what means?" And he said, "I will go out, and will be a lying spirit in the mouth of all his prophets." And he said, "You are to entice him, and you shall succeed; go out and do so.""" (1 Kings 22:19-22)

The following two scriptures show an interesting parallel suggesting relatives/ancestors in the lineage of Moses in the first scripture, and Jacob in the second:

"And die on the mountain which you go up, and be gathered to your people, as Aaron your brother died in Mount Hor and was gathered to his people." (Deuteronomy 32:50)

"Then he commanded them and said to them, 'I am to be gathered to my people; bury me with my fathers in the cave that is in the field of Ephron the Hittite.'" (Genesis 49:29)

Asking God to Take Me

Like I experienced, it is not out of the ordinary for God to take the spirit out of the body upon request when death is right at hand:

"Then they cast him out of the city and stoned him. And the witnesses laid down their garments at the feet of a young man named Saul. And as they were stoning Stephen, he called out, "Lord Jesus, receive my spirit." And falling to his knees he cried out with a loud voice, "Lord, do not hold this sin against them." And when he had said this, he fell asleep." (Acts 7:58-60)

"Then Jesus, calling out with a loud voice, said, "Father, into your hands I commit my spirit!" And having said this he breathed his last." (Luke 23:46)

Leaving My Body

The Apostle Paul reports his own out-of-body experience as well as comments on there being three heavens—the third heaven being the realm of paradise:

"I know a man in Christ who fourteen years ago was caught up to the third heaven—whether in the body or out of the body I do not know, God knows. And I know that this man was caught up into paradise—whether in the body or out of the body I do not know, God knows— and he heard things that cannot be told, which man may not utter." (2 Corinthians 12:2-4)

Part 3

Other Spiritual Encounters

9

WHAT IN HEAVEN HAS HAPPENED TO ME?

I have chosen the path of Christianity for pursuing my spirituality. But as is common with near-death experiencers, we often return with a variety of newly awakened spiritual abilities, or aftereffects. At the outset I want to say specifically that I have never pursued developing or even using any abilities I may have. The reason for this is because I am focused on the things of earth. I want to accomplish what I am here to do in this physical world, and not with any advantage or hindrance which access to the spiritual world might bring. It is important to me that my spiritual growth is not based on tapping into my ability to connect with the spiritual world, but on my development of a heartfelt relationship with God and his son through spiritual disciplines and reading the Bible.

With my two near-death experiences, I know from direct experience that my soul goes on after death. I do not need to be persuaded or convinced by any kind of further supernatural experiences. Only one time did I specifically initiate using my abilities, and as briefly discussed below, I promised myself never to do it again. All other instances I have had seeing into the spiritual world came about without my initiation.

I also want to say at the outset that these experiences are not things that happen to me daily, weekly, or even yearly. Since my first near-death experience, they have all occurred sporadically and at various times over my life. I have detected a pattern that I am especially affected around the deaths of loved ones, and others I have known throughout my life. I do not always have experiences related to deaths, though, and my experiences relate to other events and things as well.

So, in reference to all I have said thus far, after returning to earth from my first near-death experience, I gained the ability to see things in the spiritual world that I never had before. Mainly, I see spirits and visions. Also, my intuitive senses seem to be heightened. This may sound shocking or even impossible to the person who has never before heard of such things (I was shocked by it all and thought it quite impossible at first). As I later found out, many other near-death experiencers have documented an entire variety of new-found spiritual abilities as well as greater intuitive senses.

I never wondered if what I saw was just my imagination. There is a big difference between imagination and a vision. Imagination is a deliberate thought process that one can mentally visualize, manipulate and stop at will, with total control of its content and duration. A spiritual vision, though, presents itself. It is something that is seen. It unfolds on its own, and when it ends, it disappears from view. I as recipient have no control on the content or duration.

It seems evident to me now that the veil between the spiritual and natural worlds is lifted or thinned somewhat when someone has had a near-death experience. The idea of the veil is that, as human beings, we have a spirit, soul, and a body. And as human beings, we do not see readily the spiritual world all around us, though it is there. The veil is what blocks the human being from experiencing the other side, so to speak. Almost everyone can cite an example from their life when they thought they heard something, saw something, or felt something supernatural. Our culture has these ideas embedded and reflected in media such as books and movies. Human beings are not in constant awareness of the spiritual world. However, when an event happens, such as a near-death experience, that readily causes the spirit/soul to leave the body, it is as if the veil then is thinned, because you cannot unsee what you have experienced in the spirit. You now have a greater conscious awareness, because you have been there. The spirit has broken through that invisible barrier, and hence on returning to the body, your consciousness remembers and its access is not shut down or blocked as before.

The visions I have are always unexpected and can happen anywhere at any time. Usually, a quiet descends on me, which is coupled with everything around me fading away. I become totally absorbed in the vision. I simply watch. When it is over, all returns to normal as if time had been suspended. My first response is one of bewilderment, and the second is one of denial. It is difficult to believe this kind of thing can happen, but I cannot deny what I have seen. That is the dichotomy, the clash between the spiritual and natural worlds which I must deal with.

After having a vision, I try to discern any spiritual message, so I can apply it to my life and thus cope with what I have seen. When I figure that out, it is like an "Aha!" moment and gives me peace of mind, and sometimes joy. I then consider it a life lesson learned. However, I still have the denial to address. For that, I check out what I can of what I see in the vision, like certain details I have observed, when it is possible to do so. Confirmation gives the human side of me great comfort.

While I do not seek these experiences, I am humbled and awed by them and do not feel worthy to see them. I trust God my Father that these are all for my good because he wants everything that is good for all of us. They are a glimpse into the spiritual world, and I consider them a blessing and privilege to receive them. They often challenge me and stretch my understanding of our reality. In this way, my abilities do add to my personal spiritual growth.

I do have to live with what I see. Because God is good and is in control, there is always something positive to come out of the vision eventually, for which I thank him. I stand on that principle. There is also a reason for everything that happens, though I may not always know what it is. Finding it and learning from it is the goal. I then go on with my life.

The visions I document in the following chapters are the majority I have seen over my lifetime. There are, however, three experiences that I chose only to mention briefly here because I was not at the time quite sure of their meaning, and I still am not. But I want to share them as they exemplify some of the darker things I have seen.

On one occasion, I saw in my spirit a woman in a white wedding dress with a long train, instead of what she was actually wearing. This person was leaving through the door when someone standing next to me made a comment about her. Three creatures that looked like gargoyles were clinging to the dress' train. They were glaring at me and the person next to me, I assume, about that comment. Of course, no one else saw this but me. At the instant the door closed, a light bulb in a chandelier above us flared, popped and burst into shards of glass all over the floor as if in retaliation. This chandelier was not on at the time.

On another occasion, I saw the spirit of a deceased person walk out of her own funeral. The person looked like a stick figure and disappeared through a door that was not there in reality. Another spirit hovered near her and went right along with her as if attached in some way. This is the instance where I had initiated seeing a vision. I was so disconcerted by what I saw that I promised myself I would never do so again. And I have not.

On a third occasion, I had a vision while walking to my car. I saw someone dying on her bathroom floor with a glass of water that was spilled near her. She was lamenting and saying, "No," over and over again. Three dark, shadowy spirits were also there. The dark spirits pulled her downward through the floor, and they all disappeared. I was able to confirm later that this person passed away just as I had seen in the vision.

To me, these three visions remain a mystery as to why I was shown them. But like with all the visions, I have to come to terms with them and then let them go. I must let them rest with only partial understanding.

These visions, and all that follow below, to me still seem to be remarkable and unusual occurrences. They are not anything I ever imagined I would experience in my lifetime.

My many spiritual experiences follow—spanning the heights of joy to the depths of sadness, and from the greatest excitement to the sheerest terror.

10

My Neighbor's Golden Glow

Before I was married and still living with my mother, one of our neighbors died suddenly. One night around midnight, my mother awakened me with the news that our neighbor, John, had just had a heart attack and died. His wife, Sandy, was waiting for the ambulance and asked if we could come over. We were all shocked. He had no known heart condition.

I was the first to arrive. Sandy said that John's body was in their bedroom. I walked to their bedroom and looked in the door. I was startled yet amazed to see a soft, golden glow radiating all around him on the bed where he lay. The covers were pulled up to his chest, and his eyes were closed. It was a hushed, reverent scene. All I could think was that the glow surrounding him meant the area was holy. I did not feel like it would be right to step into the room, so I just stood there. A moment later, someone approached the bedroom and walked right in. My eyes followed him, and then the glow was now no longer visible to me.

This was the first vision I ever had. I wondered why I had seen what I did. On the one hand, it troubled me. On the other hand, it comforted me because it meant he was in heaven. We all adored John. He always looked out for us, it being only my mother and me. We all missed him.

Shortly before he died, Sandy and John happened to be at our house one evening when my boyfriend had arrived to pick me up for a date. They all chatted for a couple of minutes. Then John said to my boyfriend, "When are you going to marry that girl?" Well, that was a very surprising comment, and we all laughed it off. But that was John looking out for me. Not long thereafter, my boyfriend and I got engaged and then married. I wish John had been alive to enjoy the festivities. But, if he watched from heaven, I know he was happy.

11

My Unborn Child

I had a stunning vision of and interaction with my unborn child during pregnancy. The pregnancy was a difficult one. The doctor recommended plenty of rest. I did not know if I would be able to carry this child to term.

One day, when I was about three months along in my pregnancy, I went to my bedroom to rest for a while. I lay there with my eyes closed but was not asleep. After a few minutes passed, I opened my eyes. To my surprise, a child was standing at the end of my bed. I could not tell if it was a girl or a boy because of the bowl-like haircut. The child looked to be about four years old, had dark brown hair and large dark brown eyes. I was quite startled to see this.

A large warrior angel accompanied the child. He was standing at the left end corner of my bed in a protective stance. He had on a black helmet. His shoulders were so broad in his black gear that he reminded me of a football player wearing shoulder pads. He was in shadow as compared to the child, who was not. He looked toward the door of my bedroom, which was open, as if on guard against anyone coming through it.

Somehow, the angel communicated to me in my mind that this was my child who wanted to see who its mother would be in order to decide whether or not to be born. God had granted the child this special request. My focus then turned to the child.

I responded to the serious expression in the child's eyes by saying in my mind, *I will always be there for you and will never do anything hurtful.* The child seemed to take this into consideration and think then that it would be able to overcome any obstacles. And then the two of them were gone. I wondered what the child's decision would ultimately be.

As the pregnancy continued on, I reasoned that the child must have made the decision to be born. My husband and I really wanted this baby, so this made me very happy.

I delivered my baby on the exact due date. The baby had dark brown hair, as well as blue eyes that turned dark brown in a couple of weeks.

While in the recovery room in the hospital, a woman was brought in who had lost her baby and was crying loudly. It had died in utero early in her pregnancy and had just been delivered. She was inconsolable. I felt so sorry for her. I could not help but think that it could have been me.

As time passed, I forgot about the vision. But years later, I found a picture of this child at four years old with the very same bowl-like haircut the child had in the vision. How remarkable that I actually saw what my child looked like even before being born.

12

A Comforting Angel

My youngest son learned to ride a two-wheel bike with training wheels in two weeks when he was three years old. After about a month, he begged to have the training wheels removed. I did not want them removed because he was so young, even though they no longer touched the ground when he rode the bike. But my husband convinced me that we should remove them.

A few months passed with no mishaps. My boys loved riding their bikes. They would ride on our driveway or the sidewalk and sometimes across the street on the sidewalk with their friends.

One Saturday afternoon, one of their neighborhood friends set up a ramp, and the boys took turns riding over it. This was not the first time they were allowed to participate, and it really was not all that dangerous.

My husband and I were sitting in our family room when, all of a sudden, our older son came running into the house. He excitedly exclaimed in a scared voice that his brother had fallen off his bike and was dead: "He's dead! He's dead!" My husband jumped up and rushed out of the room immediately with our son at his heels.

I, on the other hand, was stunned into immobility for a moment. I soon stood up but could hardly breathe because I was so shocked and horrified. I remember putting my hand over my heart because I actually thought I was going to have a heart attack.

Then suddenly, an angel appeared before me in my family room, between me and the patio doors where the sun was shining. He said to me, "He is not dead. He is alive." I immediately believed him and felt a sense of relief. His words comforted me. He instilled no fear in me. And I did not even feel surprised. He was just there, and I never doubted his word. He gave me a wonderful message that just may have saved me from cardiac arrest.

I looked up at him as he spoke to me. My first impression was that he was large and so tall, and that I must take a good look at him because seeing an angel may never happen to me again. As I began to look him over, he stood there looking at me. His head was higher than the ceiling, but instead of going through the ceiling, which is what I expected to see, the ceiling molded itself up and around his head to accommodate his height. His wings seemed to grow out of his spine starting at his neck, curving up and away from his face, then arcing from his face down along his body to his feet. His feet were covered by his wings. He was clothed in a long garment which was a light to medium brown color. A cord was tied around his waist, and the two ends dangled down. Except for that, it was like I was looking at the negative of a photograph. There seemed to be a bright light behind him. The tips of his wings were black. The light behind him filtered through the outer fringes of his feathered wings.

Although he was looking right at me, and I at him, I cannot describe his facial features, even though I saw them. I only remember his eyes and that he had stern features. He was very calm and waited patiently while I looked him over.

All this took but a few moments because I heard the front door open and my husband quickly walking to the family room. When he came through the door, I turned my head and saw that he was carrying our son, who was very much alive. I wondered at that moment if my husband could see the angel, but when I looked back to see if the angel was still there, he was gone. The ceiling also had returned back to normal.

As for my son, he was fine but had wrecked his bike. An adult neighbor who saw it happen went to him and told him not to move, in case he had broken a bone. His brother only saw that he wasn't moving and, in his sweet innocence, thought he was dead and ran home. What a traumatic moment for all of us. I was so thankful he was all right and unharmed by his fall. Also, I was delighted and awed not only to see the angel but to be privileged to remember enough to describe him. I did not tell anyone about the angel. Who would have believed me? I can still hardly believe it myself.

13

Curious Onlookers

The time came when my husband and I decided to be baptized, that is, immersed in water baptism at our new church. The pastor did it privately. We both had been baptized as infants and wanted to do it as our own decision as adults. The following Sunday at the regular church service, the pastor introduced us to the congregation. I remember being very happy about that event. It was a long time coming after my two near-death experiences and all the spiritual life lessons.

While we were being introduced, I stood looking at the pastor and my husband. My eyes then wandered away to the ceiling where I saw a ledge. Peering over the ledge and watching us, I saw what looked like very young angels with chubby faces and wings all clustered together. That was all I could see of them. My impression was that they were curious and interested as they watched, as if they were learning about something they had never seen before. And then it was time for us to take our seats. Thinking about them makes me smile at their sweet and innocent visage.

I never told anyone about it as, like many of my spiritual experiences and visions, it was difficult for me to believe what I had seen. I tucked it away and forgot about it, but the memory stayed with me with great clarity.

14

SPIRITS IN MY HOUSE

My Closet

When my husband became ill with a progressive illness, the time came where he moved into the spare bedroom, and a hospital bed was installed. It elevated his upper body and helped him breathe better even though he was on oxygen. I slept in the master bedroom, and every night around 3:00 a.m. I would get up and check on him. I woke up automatically after a while. (After he was gone, it took me three years before I could sleep past that 3:00 a.m. hour.)

One night after I had gone to bed, I was trying to fall asleep but was having a hard time. I opened my eyes at some point only to see a man walk out of the large, main closet in my bedroom. He had on a long raincoat and a fedora which was pulled down low on his forehead. I was astonished and did not move. He did not look at me, but walked out of the closet and out the bedroom door. I was afraid he would turn his head and look at me and have red eyes, but he never turned around.

I knew he was not a flesh and blood person, but a spirit. I also knew that he would not be back. He was leaving. He disappeared into nothingness once he walked through my bedroom door. I never saw him again.

The Second Bedroom

My husband's illness kept him from working, so he stayed at home. My retirement was coming soon. He was able to take care of himself and called me every day at work, or I called him. Our daughter also called him every day as well, just to make sure he was all right.

One day when I came home after work, he had a story to tell me. He had been sitting in the living room when the spirit of a woman came out of his bedroom. She floated past him and went directly to the door leading to the deck and through it. She did not speak to him or look at him. She did not communicate with him in any way. He never saw her again. We both had now seen a spirit in the house who left and never came back.

My Front Door

On four separate occasions, I heard people talking at my front door. The first time, I innocently went to the door and opened it, but there was no one there. No one was even around.

The second time, I was more cautious and looked through the sidelights alongside the door, but once again, no one was there.

The next time I heard them, I was afraid, and did not go immediately to the door. I told myself it was just the rustling of leaves that sounded like people talking. When I finally got up the courage to go to the door, there were no leaves.

The final time it happened, I had a friend over. We were in the living room talking when I once again heard what sounded like the rustling of leaves, or people talking outside my front door. I could never make out what they were saying in the past, and I could not now. I could tell that my friend also heard it because we both paused and listened for a moment. It sounded to me like the door opened, and I heard a small group of people talking and laughing and having a good time as they walked through the foyer to the back of the house. And then all the activity ceased, and all was quiet once again. It all happened so quickly that we simply resumed our conversation, and I did not mention what we had heard. It seems that these beings had been here all along, and our presence drove them out. It was a most uncanny experience. But they were gone, and that was what mattered. That was the last of this kind of activity.

15

MY MOTHER'S DEATH

My mother developed Alzheimer's disease in her later years and eventually had to be placed in a nursing home, much to the regret of our family. Ultimately, the time came when she died. I remember the day well. I was at work when I received the dreaded phone call—she was dying, and I should come right away. My place of employment was an hour's drive away. By the time I got there, she had passed.

On arrival, one of the nurses walked me into her room. She explained that my mother had developed pneumonia. Because of her advanced Alzheimer's, she had become very fragile. There was little they could do for her but keep her comfortable. She assured me she had been with her when she died and had held her hand. I thanked her for everything. She left the room to give me some personal time with my mother.

I stood at the foot of the bed and just looked at her through my tears. Finally, I calmed myself and stayed where I was, just looking at her. All of a sudden, I heard a roaring in my ears and saw a white, flat, thin substance in a somewhat irregular shape floating about three or four inches above her. I thought perhaps it was her spirit. I was very calm and not a bit afraid at what I was seeing. As I stood there, I looked above her head and instead of the wall, I saw the earth sitting in the sky. The earth was split open a little bit, having the appearance of a wedged portion removed from it. Through the opening and around it, the sky was radiant with the colors of a beautiful sunset.

Then the roaring sound in my ears stopped, and I felt like I had just awakened from sleep. Looking around the room, my mother and everything in the room was back to normal. I was perplexed. What had I just seen and why? There was no fear associated with what I had seen. I was calm, but felt sadness at the loss of my mother, whom I dearly loved. The serenity emanating from the sunset's beautiful colors radiating in the sky comforted me and was a fitting symbol to the end of her life. I never told anyone what I saw, as this belonged to me.

16

My Husband's Death

My husband had been very ill for some time with a progressive illness. He was admitted to the hospital in the hope to see if there was anything that could help him. One night around 10:00 p.m., the nurses came to tell me that his internal systems were failing. His heart was erratic. He was dying. For the past year he had continually told me that he wished to be cremated, but I did not think I could do that to him. No one in our family had ever been cremated. I finally agreed, but only because it was what he wanted.

I called our children, and they came immediately to the hospital. We were all around his bed when he passed. A little after as we stood there, I asked them how they would feel about their dad being cremated. I was hoping they would say no, but they said yes. As we were discussing it, I was at the end of the bed by my husband's feet. As one of my sons was speaking, I saw a red ball appear in front of my husband's forehead. This was not in the physical dimension as no one else saw it. Suddenly, the red ball came towards me forcefully as the children were talking about and agreeing to his cremation. I jerked my head back just as it stopped mere inches from my forehead. The red ball then disappeared. I never told my children about it until much later. They remembered seeing me flinch but saw nothing.

At the time it happened, I wondered what it meant. I decided my husband was getting my attention at just the time his children were agreeing to his cremation. That was not a coincidence. With that, I felt I had no choice but to honor his wish. After all, I told him that I would. He was cremated and rests in peace.

I gave instructions to the crematorium to call my daughter when they had completed the cremation. I really did not want to talk with them about it. I would be better able to hear that news if it came from her. But did that happen? No. They called me. I phoned my daughter to let her know so she would not wait for their call. She felt bad about it, but I suppose that was how it was meant to be.

That night around 1:30 a.m., I received a phone call from her. She said she had awakened to the presence of her father in the room and a tingling feeling all over her body. She wondered what that meant. I told her it was her father's love for her. Since it was her practice to call him each day while I was at work to check on him, I thought perhaps he was checking on her to make sure that she was all right.

That same night at 3:00 a.m., I woke up to see him in spirit come into my bedroom. It was his essence that I sensed, his spirit, the real him. He had checked on our daughter, and now he was checking on me. He was just making sure I was all right, too. Or perhaps he was just saying a final goodbye to both of us.

We really do not die—we just move into another realm and state of being. Our spirits live forever. I am sure that my husband is happy in heaven, and that comforts me. There will come a day, I know, when I will see him again. It will be a joyous celebration. I thank God for all the years we had together, and I look forward to going through eternity with him and all my loved ones.

17

THE DEATH OF A CHILDHOOD FRIEND

When I was in my 50s, I was reacquainted with a dear childhood friend who grew up with me in my neighborhood. Their family had moved to California after grade school, and she had now moved back to the area after all these years. Alice and I met for coffee and lunch several times. I enjoyed our visits.

One day, I invited Alice over for lunch. Just before sitting down to eat, I happened to glance over at the front door only to see a spirit standing in my house. I understood it to be one of her deceased relatives. A second one of her deceased relatives was standing behind the first. The first spirit was pointing at something. My spirit must have gone from me to where they were standing because I was suddenly right next to them. I looked to where the first spirit was pointing, and I saw a road. The road was strewn with debris. I looked down the road and saw that it came to a dead end. And then the vision was over. It lasted what seemed like less than a minute. I did not understand what it meant. I said nothing to Alice about it.

A few days later, the second deceased relative returned and stood next to an open door to one of the rooms in my house. The spirit seemed angry with me and said that I wasn't being serious enough with Alice. As always, when I encounter a vision, I do not have any interest or intent to interact with a spirit. I simply watch and observe. His angry words were surprising. I did not quite know what to make of it. I decided that God had allowed it to happen for some reason. Therefore, the next time we met, we did talk about my near-death experience. We also discussed God and religion. I did this because I believed this was what God would have wanted. If she did not want to talk about it, I would have dropped the subject.

After all these things happened, I had not heard from her for quite a while. I was concerned. Somehow, I got the feeling something was wrong.

I eventually found out that Alice had passed away, and right around the time I began to be concerned about her. I was so sorry to hear that. In retrospect, I was glad I shared my near-death experience with her, and that we had spiritually oriented conversations. I then knew why the two spirits visited me and showed such serious concern. I never saw either of those spirits again.

18

AN ANGEL AT A FUNERAL

I was at a funeral service for a longtime friend's spouse. Suddenly, as the priest raised the host to consecrate it, I saw an angel standing a few feet away from him, a little to the left of the altar. The angel was formidable in size with a graceful form and wings. There was a glow in front of him as he observed the ritual. (In retrospect, I am not sure whether the glow came from him or the ceiling lights reflected off the floor.) His demeanor was such that he seemed to approve the ritual because of the sincerity of the priest and his adulation of the host. Then the vision ended.

The whole scene was one of reverence. I was astonished and felt blessed to have seen it. It seemed here that God was honoring the deceased person and the priest. He sent an angel to the funeral mass just at those specific few moments that expressly honored his son.

The message I took from this is that God honors those who have a genuine heartfelt love for him and have a personal relationship with his son. This, to me, was an example of that. It was what I had lacked at the time of my first near-death experience. I am assuming that is why I was privileged to see this brief vision.

19

A SPIRIT MASKING AS MY MOTHER

After gaining a few pounds, I decided one day to try a popular diet to lose them. To my delight, the diet worked. I decided to continue it for just one more week.

To my regret, I found that well into the second week, I awoke one morning and just did not have the energy to get out of bed. As I lay there waiting for my strength to return, I noticed a movement to my left. I looked over to see my mother looking at me as she walked toward the wall that faced my bed. Now, my mother had been dead for several years.

While looking at me, she beckoned me to follow her. I wondered to myself why she would do that. I wasn't dying, or was I? This all seemed wrong somehow. She looked away from me for a moment and then looked back. To my surprise, it was not her face I saw. It was that of an evil spirit with a malevolent leer on his face, as if he had put something over on me, which he had. He then turned his head forward toward the wall and disappeared through it. I was horrified at what I saw. Since I recognized it as a vision, I knew I had nothing to fear, but I did not like it one bit.

Shortly thereafter, I gathered up enough strength to get out of bed. I went into my kitchen and ate something sweet to give me energy. I called work to say I would not be in that day and went back to bed to rest. By evening time, and after eating whatever I felt like, my strength returned, and I felt much better. I decided the whole experience was not worth the few pounds lost.

I did not discuss the vision with anyone at that time nor for a long time after. I did not really think anyone else would look at it the way I had. They would probably think I hallucinated.

From a human point of view, I learned that since I was already on a sugar restricted food plan because of my particular food allergies, any other diet I might adhere to in addition was not a good idea. Combining them was a mistake, and mistakes lead us down the wrong road, compounding the error.

From a spiritual point of view, evil spirits sometimes take advantage of our mistakes and use them as an opportunity to deceive us. This evil spirit did that by impersonating my mother and beckoning me to follow her to make me think I could be dying. However, I knew my mother would never do anything like that. Also, except for the one moment that I questioned myself about dying, I knew I was not. He tricked me into thinking I could be, though. That is when he showed me his leering face and disappeared leaving me horrified over the whole incident.

This experience resulted in my determination to stick to the food plan created especially for me, and that one only. I will live a healthier life doing so. That was the lesson learned and the good that came out of the vision.

20

AN ANGEL'S OFFER

One of our old neighbors, with whom my husband and I still kept in contact, had been very ill for some time with a terminal disease. Paul was a good soul and loved life, even though I know he suffered greatly. One morning while I was at home, I had a vision of him as he sat on the edge of his bed. His head was bent down, and an angel hovered alongside him. The angel asked him, "Do you want to be healed?" I understood the angel to mean that if Paul was ready to die, in death he would find healing from his pain. The angel was bending forward toward him as if he was trying to comfort him with those words, but Paul shook his head to say no. And then the vision was over.

I noted that in the vision I saw a very unique picture frame that was hanging on the wall to the left of where they were positioned. I wondered if it really existed. My humanity always wants to deny what I have seen, but I cannot lie to myself, so I have to cope with the inevitable opposition. I checked with Paul's wife to see if the unique picture frame was in that spot, and she said it was.

Personally, I was surprised Paul did not take the angel up on his offer. If he had, he would have been free from the pain. In not doing so, he certainly showed his love and devotion to his family and was not yet ready to leave them.

An Angel's Offer

Apparently, some have a choice whether to live or die when they are that ill. Perhaps God chose to give him a little more time to be able to endure the pain until he was ready for the inevitable. I consider this to be a tender mercy from God who honored Paul's desire because he loved him. He passed away shortly thereafter. We were devastated for his family at the news, even though expected, but happy for him that he was finally free from the pain and healed.

21

You Are Sealed

Reading a book about the biblical feast days given to the Israelites in the Old Testament piqued my interest. I attended a Messianic Jewish service on the day of the Feast of Trumpets. I wanted to hear the sound of the shofar, and enjoyed the experience. A few years later, my interest in the feast days returned. This time, I wanted to honor God by experiencing another of his appointed times for the Jewish nation. I chose the Day of Atonement.

When that day came, I fasted, prayed, tried to remember my sins, and confessed them to God. The Israelites did this once a year to have their sins forgiven for that particular year. I did not know if I would be able to fast for 24 hours but wanted to try. To my surprise, I was able to do it and was happy about that.

Upon awaking the next morning, I opened my eyes to find an angel standing in my bedroom. He was about ten feet away from me. I immediately sat up, and we just looked at each other. He reminded me of a young man perhaps in his twenties. Except for the quizzical expression on his face, my memory is blocked from any other description of him. He paused for a moment while looking at me, and then his countenance became serious. He was looking closely at my forehead. Like someone who was doing his job, I heard him say in my mind, "You are sealed." And then he disappeared. I was very shocked by all of this. I wondered what was going on, and why he had been sent to me. None of this was even remotely expected.

I was happy to know that I was sealed, but his expression of puzzlement bewildered me. Did he, in looking at my forehead at that moment, realize that I was sealed already, and thus tell me I was sealed? Or did he seal me at some moment and then tell me what he had done? Did every person who observed that day also have a visit by an angel with perhaps a similar message? I can't imagine that would be true. I could not figure out any of this, so I set the vision aside. I could not deal with it.

Sometime later, thoughts of this vision returned to me. It was time to come to terms with it. The angel said the words to me, "You are sealed," because most likely he saw I was already sealed. That was the reason why he looked puzzled, and why he hesitated. It is hard for me to understand that he would not know this already before coming to visit me. Regardless, he delivered the message he was sent to deliver.

The Bible teaches that those who believe in Jesus are sealed with the Holy Spirit. Ephesians 1:13-14 says, "In him you also, when you heard the word of truth, the gospel of your salvation, and believed in him, were sealed with the promised Holy Spirit, who is the guarantee of our inheritance until we acquire possession of it, to the praise of his glory." A seal is something that confirms, ratifies, makes secure, guarantees, assures, certifies, or authenticates something. The presence of the Holy Spirit is the seal.

As far as my desire and actions to honor and participate in the Day of Atonement, there was no need, as I am already saved for eternity. Jesus completed all the Old Testament requirements for salvation and set us free from the Law of Moses.

It is likely that God sent the angel to me as a confirmation that I was already sealed and to keep to the Christian path. The puzzlement on the angel's face seems to confirm that. Apparently, I was meant to see his puzzlement. It was the reason I had to think about it to come to terms with it.

The comfort and love I now felt within me to finally understand and appreciate the meaning of the vision overcame my discomfort over the experience: I am sealed.

22

Two Slithery Spirits

I had just gone to bed and was having trouble falling asleep. I sat up to adjust my pillows. The room was unusually dark. Shockingly and suddenly, a spirit in the form of a dark green snake came up out of the darkness and hovered near the end of my bed. I could only make out its face, which was very large. It had indentations on either side of its head that pushed its skin up a bit and looked like ears. I noticed this because I did not think snakes had ears. I was so disturbed that I could barely move. The snake had dark green scales that looked flat and silky smooth. Although it was a horrible sight, it also had a kind of beauty to it. As if it heard my thought, I sensed it wanted me to extend my hand to touch it, trying to tempt me, but I would not and did not.

Just then, another snake appeared slightly behind and alongside the first snake, which increased my horror. It appeared curious, as if wondering what was going on here. Then in my mind, I heard the first snake ask if it could enter into me, as if to take up a dwelling inside me or attach itself to me in some way. I shook my head no. I would have verbally said "No!" but I could not speak because I was so frightened.

I lowered my head for a moment in disbelief at what was happening. At this moment, I felt a warm, loving, and protective presence behind me. It seemed to shore me up. I then looked up and started to take a breath. To my astonishment, a very powerful, bright white light came up from within me and seemed to come out of my mouth. It was a very fast flash of bright light, like a camera flash. I saw the first snake's reaction, and it was one of having been rebuked. It could not stand the light. Both snakes immediately slithered back together into the darkness and disappeared.

It seems that evil lurks everywhere and is frightful. I cannot say exactly what I did or how I did it, but it must have been the Holy Spirit within me. In any event, whatever it was, I give it up to the protection and glory of God.

The snakes have never come back, nor have I ever again had such an experience.

23

Charismatic Church Visit

Early on in my quest to find my place in God's church, I visited a Catholic charismatic church where they practiced the gift of speaking in tongues and baptizing people in the Holy Spirit. I had both Protestant and Catholic friends who were in the Charismatic movement. In this church, the priest would lay his hands on someone, say a prayer, then touch their forehead and they would fall backward. Someone would catch them and gently place them on the floor, as they seemed to blackout for a few seconds.

I decided I wanted to be "baptized in the Spirit," too. The priest put his hands on me, prayed, and then touched my forehead. I fell backward but did not blackout. I lay there quietly for a moment without moving and then got up. I was not sure about all this.

The result of the experience was that I acquired my own "angel" language, like the Apostle Paul reports in the Bible. I was given only one sentence. I did not know what it meant then and do not know what it means now. I assume it simply praised God.

As I sat in a pew in that same church during a service, a man stood up and gave a message in a tongue. When I heard him speak, my mind automatically interpreted it into English, and I understood what he said. It surprised me. When the priest asked for a show of hands from anyone who could translate the message, several people raised their hands, including me. I wondered if my interpretation was correct and was willing to take the chance. Someone else was called on.

Everyone listened to the person's interpretation, and no one challenged him on his understanding. I do not remember the exact wording he used, but it was a positive message addressed to the church as a whole. It was not exactly as I heard it in my mind, but the gist of the message was the same.

As I continued on with my friends in this movement for a short time, I became more and more uncomfortable with it. It just was not for me. I still had not found what I was looking for.

Time passed, and this experience melted into the mist of forgetfulness as I continued to move forward, always forward, to an unknown goal. I wondered if I would ever find what I was looking for.

This experience brings up an important question. Did I receive an ability to understand spiritual tongues because I had been "baptized in the Spirit," or did I have this ability already as an aftereffect of my near-death experience? I do not know the answer. This was the only time this happened to me, and I never sought any such experiences afterward.

24

BABY GENDER AND NAME

What a surprise! On Mother's Day a few years ago, my son and his wife visited me and handed me two envelopes. The first one was a lovely Mother's Day card. The second one stunned me. It was a sonogram picture of a baby! I was overjoyed.

My family was excited with the good news. We of course wondered if it would be a girl or a boy, and what its name would be.

One day well into the pregnancy, my son asked me whether I thought they would have a boy or a girl. I didn't have an inkling. A week or so later, I was in my car driving somewhere, I don't remember where, and out of the blue the name "Little Bobby" came into my head. Why did that pop into my head? I was not thinking about the baby at the time, but when something like that happens, I know to pay attention. I had to laugh at the "Little Bobby" moniker. Is it a boy, I wondered? I bet it is, I thought, and all I could do was smile.

When we next spoke, he again asked if I thought they would have a girl or a boy. Since I really could not believe that I thought it was a boy because of what I had heard in my head, I said, is it a girl? He said no, it's a boy. I asked if they had picked out a name yet. They were working on that but had not yet made a decision. I didn't tell him until a later date what I had heard in my car.

When I prayed about my son's baby, I wondered if God would tell me his name. I did not specifically ask him for it. However, I remembered that one time I had actually dreamed the name of a friend's baby girl. The first name was shown to me in picture form. The middle name was spoken to me in my mind. This turned out to be correct. Remembering this past precognitive dream, I thought maybe I would dream my new grandson's name, too. But I did not dream anything.

Some time passed since I had prayed about my son's baby, and I again began thinking about the baby boy who was not yet born. All of a sudden, I had a vision—I was at my son's house in their family room. It looked like I was babysitting, but I was looking down on him and do not think my feet were touching the floor. He was sitting on the edge of the carpet playing with wooden building blocks, placing one on top of the other on the vinyl floor adjacent to the rug. He looked to be around three years old. His back was to me, and it was very straight. He reminded me of my husband—perhaps it was the shape of his head. His hair was a little darker than his grandfather's but even so reminded me of him.

Just then his mother came home from work. I heard the front door open, and she went into my son's office. They spoke a few words, and then she peeked around the corner. I heard her very clearly call out to her son by name. Then the vision ended.

What had just happened, I wondered? Did I really see that? Of course, I know I did. I saw it and heard her voice calling out to her son by name.

Eventually I told my son about the vision. He said the name I heard was the Greek variant of the name his mother had chosen to call him. Why I heard the Greek version, I do not know. But I looked it up to verify it for myself, and it was so. In any event, my heart's desire had come true—my son was having a baby, and I was overjoyed. And now I knew his name.

God did not tell me his name, nor did I dream it. Instead, he revealed it in a vision. Even though I saw it, it is still hard to believe even now. At birth, the baby was given the name its mother had chosen, that is, the English version of the name I had heard in the vision. I am overwhelmed by God's loving kindness and am forever grateful for his blessings.

25

Conclusion

This memoir depicts forays of my life into the spirit world. As time has passed, two issues I wrote about were resolved. For one, I have read the Bible. I believe its words and follow its precepts as best I know how. And two, I finally put to rest the upset caused by my biological father's death, which happened when I was five years old. I stopped blaming God for it.

As for now, I am in the process of attempting to fulfill two other goals: one, the continual quest to grow my spirit; and two, the job assigned to me during my second near-death experience concerning the now identified mystery person symbolized by the second mountain. I continue on in my quest to help my small spirit grow into a heartfelt faith. I also continue to apply the spiritual lessons learned in both of my near-death experiences and other earthly spiritual encounters toward my current life endeavors.

I truly hope my experiences serve as evidence and encouragement in understanding that there is a God who absolutely loves us and is always there for us. He wishes to be loved in turn through worship in spirit and in truth. But we must be aware that we have a spirit in order to do that, and that it needs to be nourished in order to grow in the knowledge of God. Growth happens the more we learn about him and his savior.

Conclusion

Finally, I hope my experiences have revealed how connected we are to the heavenly realm. Our spirits come from God and will go back to him after bodily death (or during a near-death experience!). Therefore, we each must decide to live consciously aware of his love with thanks for all he has given us as we grow spiritually and move toward our eternal dwelling place. It is the most important decision any of us will ever make.

Life is certainly worth living. Our souls are our eventual passport into heaven. As we grow and strive in our humanity, the goal is to be an overcomer, particularly over the evil that comes our way. The Bible has proved for me to be the best guide to living righteously, and its tenets are worth following. Surely, following Jesus's command to love one another is the basis for growth in the spirit. The end result can be one of incomparable beauty, peace, and love for each of us. We cannot possibly fathom this love until our spirits are called home to heaven for eternity.

My fervent wish for you is a blessed life and happiness throughout eternity.

FOR MY FATHER

I walk the same streets you once walked,
My footsteps layered over yours,
And hear your voice as if you've talked,
You live inside me somewhere.

I try to feel your thoughts but can't,
Your spirit has eluded me.
Your presence is so strong at times,
It hovers everywhere.

My wandering finds me at your feet.
My lonely shadow covers you.
Above us clouds and sunrays play
As we are deeply bonded.

The days and years have passed us by.
Your love will always live in me.
I've brought a flower for your grave.
Now I must let you go.

About the Author

Tina Wrassmann is a first-generation American whose parents came through Ellis Island in the 1920s. She holds a Certificate in Business Administration, an A.A. in Liberal Arts, and a B.S. in English Literature from the University of Cincinnati. She spent most of her career in Human Resources. She has three children, and grandchildren. Since retiring, her new career is one filled with the enjoyment of reading books, traveling, spending time with friends, doting on her grandchildren, and completing the goals she has set for her life.

Made in United States
Orlando, FL
09 July 2025